FUNDAMENTALISM AND SECULARIZATION

SUSPENSIONS: CONTEMPORARY MIDDLE EASTERN AND ISLAMICATE THOUGHT

Series editors: Jason Bahbak Mohaghegh and Lucian Stone

This series interrupts standardized discourses involving the Middle East and the Islamicate world by introducing creative and emerging ideas. The incisive works included in this series provide a counterpoint to the reigning canons of theory, theology, philosophy, literature, and criticism through investigations of vast experiential typologies—such as violence, mourning, vulnerability, tension, and humour—in light of contemporary Middle Eastern and Islamicate thought.

Other titles in this series include:

Gilles Deleuze, Postcolonial Theory, and the Philosophy of Limit, Réda Bensmaïa

The Qur'an and Modern Arabic Literary Criticism: From Taha to Nasr, Mohammad Salama

Hostage Spaces of the Contemporary Islamicate World, Dejan Lukic

On the Arab Revolts and the Iranian Revolution, Arshin Adib-Moghaddam

The Politics of Writing Islam, Mahmut Mutman

The Writing of Violence in the Middle East, Jason Bahbak Mohaghegh

Iranian Identity and Cosmopolitanism, edited by Lucian Stone

Continental Philosophy and the Palestinian Question, by Zahi Zalloua

Sorcery, Totem and Jihad, Christopher Wise

Orientalism and Imperialism, Andrew Wilcox

Traces of Racial Exception, Ronit Lentin

Transgression and the Inexistent, Mehdi Belhaj Kacem

Plural Maghreb: Writings on Postcolonialism, Abdelkebir Khatibi

Revolutionary Bodies, K.S. Batmanghelichi

Contesting Islam, Constructing Race and Sexuality, Sunera Thobani

FUNDAMENTALISM AND SECULARIZATION

MOURAD WAHBA

*Translated and Edited by
Robert K. Beshara*

BLOOMSBURY ACADEMIC
LONDON • NEW YORK • OXFORD • NEW DELHI • SYDNEY

BLOOMSBURY ACADEMIC
Bloomsbury Publishing Plc
50 Bedford Square, London, WC1B 3DP, UK
1385 Broadway, New York, NY 10018, USA
29 Earlsfort Terrace, Dublin 2, Ireland

BLOOMSBURY, BLOOMSBURY ACADEMIC and the Diana logo are trademarks
of Bloomsbury Publishing Plc

First published in Great Britain 2022
This paperback edition published 2023

Copyright © Mourad Wahba and Robert K. Beshara, 2022

Mourad Wahba has asserted his right under the Copyright, Designs and
Patents Act, 1988, to be identified as Author of this work.

Robert K. Beshara has asserted his right under the Copyright, Designs and
Patents Act, 1988, to be identified as Translator and Editor of this work.

For legal purposes the Acknowledgments on p. vi constitute an extension of
this copyright page.

Cover image: Moroccan Tiles (© JayKay57 / Getty Images)

All rights reserved. No part of this publication may be reproduced or transmitted
in any form or by any means, electronic or mechanical, including photocopying,
recording, or any information storage or retrieval system, without prior
permission in writing from the publishers.

Bloomsbury Publishing Plc does not have any control over, or responsibility for,
any third-party websites referred to or in this book. All internet addresses given
in this book were correct at the time of going to press. The author and publisher
regret any inconvenience caused if addresses have changed or sites have ceased
to exist, but can accept no responsibility for any such changes.

A catalogue record for this book is available from the British Library.

Library of Congress Cataloging-in-Publication Data
Names: Wahbah, Murad, author. | Beshara, Robert K., translator.
Title: Fundamentalism and secularization / Mourad Wahba; translated and
edited by Robert K. Beshara.
Other titles: Usuliyah wa-al-almaniyah. English
Description: London; New York: Bloomsbury Academic, 2022. |
Series: Suspensions: contemporary Middle Eastern and Islamicate thought |
Includes bibliographical references and index.
Identifiers: LCCN 2021031074 (print) | LCCN 2021031075 (ebook) |
ISBN 9781350228702 (ebook) | ISBN 9781350228696 (epdf) | ISBN 9781350228689 (hb)
Subjects: LCSH: Religious fundamentalism. | Secularism.
Classification: LCC BL238 (ebook) | LCC BL238.W3413 2022 (print) | DDC 306.6–dc23
LC record available at https://lccn.loc.gov/2021031074

ISBN: HB: 978-1-3502-2868-9
PB: 978-1-3502-2872-6
ePDF: 978-1-3502-2869-6
eBook: 978-1-3502-2870-2

Series: Suspensions: Contemporary Middle Eastern and Islamicate Thought

Typeset by Deanta Global Publishing Services, Chennai, India

To find out more about our authors and books visit www.bloomsbury.com and
sign up for our newsletters.

CONTENTS

Acknowledgments vi
Foreword: An Interview with Mourad Wahba (2019) vii
Translator's Preface to the English Edition xviii
Author's Preface to the Arabic Edition (1995) xxxi

Part I Fundamentalism and Secularization

1. What Is Fundamentalism? 3
2. What Is Secularization? 42
3. Fundamentalism and Secularization in the Contemporary Middle East 57
4. Postmodernism and Fundamentalism 83

Notes 94
References 98

Part II Essays

5. The Concept of the Good in Islamic Philosophy 103
6. Philosophy in North Africa 120

Index 141

ACKNOWLEDGMENTS

This translation would not have been possible without the full encouragement of both Professor Mourad Wahba and his son, Dr. Magdy Mourad. To the Wahbas, I am eternally grateful! I also see this collaboration as the beginning of a long-term translation project of not only other books by Professor Wahba but also different contemporary classics of Arabic philosophy. I thank my editors at Bloomsbury (Liza Thompson and Lucy Russell) for believing in this effort, which makes accessible to a curious and philosophically oriented English-speaking audience a sample of North African philosophy. Finally, what would scholars do without the love and support of their family, friends, and colleagues? Many thanks to Cony Garrido (who read the manuscript a few times to check for typos), Khairy Beshara (who introduced me to the work of Mourad Wahba), Alberto Hernandez-Lemus (who introduced me to work of Sadik Al Azm, another important thinker from the Arab world), Lewis Gordon (who made me realize Wahba's significance within Africana philosophy), and Zahi Zalloua (who recommended Bloomsbury to me). Not mentioning Ian Parker, Olúfẹ́mi Táíwò, and Zeyad el Nabolsy who helped me in one way or another regarding this project.

FOREWORD

AN INTERVIEW WITH MOURAD WAHBA (2019)

Robert Beshara: Please introduce yourself, Professor Mourad Wahba, for the reader who may not be familiar with your work as a philosopher.

Mourad Wahba: My philosophical school of thought is against dogmatism and for relativity as a style of thinking as opposed to a belief. Therefore, I am against saying that the mind is capable of bearing the Absolute Truth. In this context, I began researching a property, which was not being researched as much as agricultural property and industrial property. Epistemic property was not seen as significant when, in my judgment, it is more important than the other two properties, for it is the one that either supports or undermines civilizational progress. Secularization negates the grasping of the Absolute Truth; fundamentalism, on the other hand, claims the negation of this negation. Creativity ceases with fundamentalism. If creativity is the beginning of agricultural technique, which is the reason civilization exists, then the human must be defined as a creative animal first and a social animal second. And if creativity knows no limits then the mind, by default, transcends limits and is capable, consequently, of forming a rational cosmic vision—a vision that permits, in its formation, three unified sciences: physics, politics, and philosophy. The natural sciences are embedded within physics, the social and human sciences are part of politics, and philosophy unites the first two sciences. Since these three sciences begin with the letter *P* in English, then one can call them the three *P* sciences.

RB: Your book, *Fundamentalism and Secularization*, was published in 1995 but it remains relevant to this day in 2019, and, in my opinion, will remain relevant for the foreseeable future. In many ways, I see it as a visionary work of philosophy and theory because the book unpacks and historicizes significant concepts and also deals with important social issues six years before the tragic events on 9/11 and George W. Bush's subsequent launch of the "war on terror," which is, of course, ongoing. Having said that, what inspired you to write the book? How was it received in 1995? And how do you think it will be received today, especially as an English translation? How do you feel about the translation and the possibility of this book reaching a wider audience now?

MW: Dr. Rev. Samuel Habib, the president of the Protestant Churches of Egypt, is the one who drove me to write this book after my conversations with him and with other Reverends, who belong to this denomination [i.e., Coptic Evangelical Organization for Social Services or CEOSS]. He felt that I held a futuristic vision that involved new terms and which was worthy of being published on a large scale. Therefore, it was natural for the book to be released through *Dar El Thaqafa* [The House of Culture], which belongs to CEOSS. The paradox here is that neither the print media nor broadcast media commented upon the book. Moreover, a second edition was never published despite the book selling out. However, I expect the English translation of this book will become popular and widespread throughout the Western world, which currently suffers from a religious terrorism, spawned from religious fundamentalisms. One can even say that the translator, Dr. Robert Beshara, is the author of the English version of this book, especially since he has a command of both English and Arabic.

RB: One of the most impressive aspects of the book is your mastery of both Euro-American philosophy and Arab-Islamic philosophy. Not only that, you synthesize the continental and the analytic traditions in Euro-American philosophy very smoothly. I have not seen any other author seamlessly bridging these philosophical or cultural traditions like you do, which is one of the reasons why I took it upon myself to translate this wonderful book. I am convinced by your argument that there is only *one human civilization and many cultures*, which is basically a critique of Samuel P. Huntington's "clash of civilizations" hypothesis. Edward Said was also critical of Huntington's hypothesis, and he opted for two alternative phrases: "clash of ignorance" and "clash of definitions." Would you tell us more about your hypothesis and how it informs not just this book but your other works as well? And how do you situate this book in the context of your other writings?

MW: My argument is a result of my dedication to reading as well as writing without interruption for over thirty-seven years in addition to my personal conversations with world philosophers and my participation in organizing regional as well as international conferences. In this context, I became aware that there is only *one human civilization and many cultures*. In this sense, I held an international philosophy conference with that title, and I came to this conclusion as a rebuttal to the "clash of civilizations" hypothesis, which was promoted by Samuel Huntington (1996) in his book *The Clash of Civilizations and the Remaking of World Order*. The purpose of my idea is promoting intercultural dialogue so that all cultures come near the path of one civilization, putting an end to the clash. This idea led to another idea, which is that in every society there are two conditions: the status quo and the pro quo. When the status quo enters into a crisis, a challenge is posed to this status quo, which consists of a futuristic vision that has the potential for eliminating the crisis-ridden existing state of affairs and transferring it to the past, whereby it becomes heritage. Therefore, heritage cannot be the beginning since it was originally a pro quo that later called for an alternative to a crisis-ridden existing state of affairs and then went into hiding afterwards in what is called bygone. From here arose my conception of time, whence priority is given to the future and not to the past. If we desire to revive the past, then it should only be the part that was deprived from its futuristic vision. Ibn Rushd, for example, is dead in the East, yet alive in the West. This is the paradox of Ibn Rushd, which brought about a development in how I see both the twentieth century and this century.

RB: The book has a number of original ideas, such as the organic relationship between religious fundamentalism and what you call "parasitic capitalism," which I understand essentially as financialization in the context of neoliberalism beginning in the late

1970s. Again, your book was published before the financial crisis of 2008, which is one of the clearest examples of the effects of parasitic capitalism. Do you want to comment on this?

MW: My comment is as follows: I discovered the organic relationship between fundamentalism and parasitic capitalism in the mid-1970s, and I confirmed it during my conversation with an economics professor from Harvard University in 1976 when he said: "We deliberately established this relationship to destroy the public sector in Egypt and in order to establish a private sector." My reply was that this destructive relationship would not permit the establishment of the private sector because parasitic values, in Egypt's case, would have controlled society, and parasitism is something that contradicts with the desire for establishing a private sector. Furthermore, I discovered afterwards that this organic relationship was becoming widespread globally under the leadership of the American intelligence service, which admitted—in a publicly released statement after the end of the Soviet-Afghan War—that they were selling drugs in order to buy weapons.

RB: What you write about the "New Right" is so prescient because the current "Alt-Right" movement is but a revival of the New Right. What do you think of the rise of right-wing politics around the world over the last few years?

MW: The rise of the New Right is nothing but a support for religious fundamentalism; however, this expression reminds one of the binary division between the Right and the Left that prevailed during the Cold War, but no longer resonates now given the collapse of the Communist Bloc.

RB: Related to the previous question, you show that Edmund Burke is perhaps the first theorist of fundamentalism. To me this suggests that not only is secularization the antidote to fundamentalism but also the fruit of revolution. Is this not the implication of your thesis?

MW: You are correct to say this because Burke was against the French Revolution.

RB: Another dialectic that you explore in the book, which I find fascinating, is the relationship between religious fundamentalism and postmodernism. You regard the two as structurally similar in many ways because of their rejection of modernism, particularly the method of textual interpretation. I think that is a unique argument because most scholars might situate religious fundamentalism in premodernity, but you actually show that it is a postmodern phenomenon. This is very similar to Adam Curtis's (2004) argument in *The Power of Nightmares*, wherein he compares the neoconservative movement in the United States with Islamic extremism. While the two are officially enemies, Curtis argues that a certain ideological fantasy structures both of their programs. Curtis focuses, in particular, on Sayyid Qutb and Leo Strauss. Any comments?

MW: No comment because you agree with me that there is an organic relationship between fundamentalism and postmodernism.

RB: I am curious if you have considered the works of decolonial thinkers, like Enrique Dussel, who make the case for transmodernity, or cultures that are exterior to (post)modernity, and that should be considered on their own terms and not according to a developmental model set by Euro-America. Decoloniality challenges the Euro-American conception of temporality and progress. What are your thoughts on that, particularly in relation to fundamentalism?

MW: I began dealing with Enrique Dussel since I met him in a philosophy conference in Bogotá, the capital of Colombia. But I discovered that the call to fight colonialism is, in fact, a call to fight Enlightenment on grounds that we need to transcend modernity toward postmodernity. Liberation theology, which Dussel promotes, is a counter-Enlightenment theology. For this reason, I stopped dealing with him.

RB: In his book *The Great Theft*, Khaled Abou El Fadl (2005, pp. 18–19) makes an argument against using the term "fundamentalism." Instead, he prefers to call groups like Al Qaeda or the Islamic State in Iraq and the Levant (ISIL) as puritanical, extremist, fanatic, or radical. What are your thoughts? Why not use these other terms, and why should we continue to characterize religious terrorists as fundamentalists?

MW: I think the terms "Puritanism," "extremism," "fanaticism," and "radicalism" are vague expressions, which have been circulating over the ages. Therefore, their use produces a generalization concerning the phenomenon of fundamentalism, which is a phenomenon specific to the twentieth century and beyond. Also, fundamentalism precisely determines the enemy's nature. The fundamentalist is a terrorist, in my estimation, since terrorism is the highest stage of religious fundamentalisms.

RB: Some scholars are critical of secularism when it functions as an ideology in Euro-America in the sense of becoming just an implicit or cultural form of Judeo-Christianity that is not tolerant of other cultures or religions, particularly Islam. This is quite clear in the case of France, with *laïcité*, where there is a ban on the expression of religious symbols in public spaces. However, that law seems to be targeting Muslims more than any other group. This led some scholars, like Rosi Braidotti (2008) in her article *In Spite of the Times: The Postsecular Turn in Feminism*, to think of a critical space that is postsecular, which for her is a specifically feminist space. What do you think of this postsecular argument?

MW: Saying that secularization is the "cultural form of Judeo-Christianity that is not tolerant of other cultures or religions, particularly Islam" is a statement that implies a historical fallacy because after the spread of the Latin Averroism and subsequent European secularization—not mentioning what secularization prompted in terms of resistance from the Judeo-Christian authorities—Europe became divided against itself. Consequently, secularization entered into a crisis, so what is needed is the sovereignty of secularization and not postsecularism.

RB: Other scholars who have problematized the question of secularism from a critical perspective include Talal Asad, Wendy Brown, Judith Butler, and Saba Mahmood (2009) in their coauthored book *Is Critique Secular? Blasphemy, Injury, and Free Speech*. In your book, you certainly complexify our understanding of secularism by pointing to the fact that secular Islam will look very different from secular Christianity or any other form of secularism; hence, why you think Ibn Rushd is crucial. Your sensitivity to history and context is a point well taken. So can you speak more about the specificity of secularism in North Africa and West Asia, and some of the challenges that you can foresee?

MW: Given that the heritage [*al-turath*] of both Christianity and Islam are different in terms of their conceptualization of secularization, the Latin Ibn Rushd will not be similar to the Islamic Ibn Rushd because interpretation, which is the essence of Islamic Averroism, happens in the context of the Arabic language and its conditions. As for interpretation in Latin Averroism, it occurs in the context of the Romance languages. Moreover, the term "secularization" is forbidden and criminalized in Islamic history. Thus, I thought that Ibn Rushd could be the gateway to secularization till it becomes acceptable, and this is the challenge, which lingers to date.

RB: Some scholars are critical of comparing Islamic revival with the Reformation in Europe claiming that groups like ISIL are essentially calling for a reformation. Therefore, these scholars argue for embracing traditional Islam since the majority of Muslims around the world are peaceful. What do you think?

MW: My opinion is that the reformation that ISIL calls for signifies reviving the Islamic Caliphate or, more precisely, the Ottoman Caliphate, and that is the opposite of what happened with the Reformation movement in Europe.

RB: Edward Said (1983) has a wonderful essay in his book *The World, The Text, and The Critic*, which is titled "Secular Criticism." Did you ever read this essay, and if so, how does it inform your understanding of secularism? I think Said's essay can be read as an ideology critique of secularism, or any -ism for that matter with the exception of criticism, which can never really become an ideology. I find his critical humanist position to be in line with your critique of the bearers of the Absolute Truth, who are also known as dogmatists or ideologues. Did Said have any influence on you?

MW: I read the writings of Edward Said and he is correct in his critique of secularism if it ends with "-ism" since, in this case, it becomes similar to the Absolute Truth. Therefore, I distinguish between secularism and secularization. The second term is better because it does not imply any absolute feature.

RB: As I was translating the last chapter in the book, I was thinking where is Ihab Hassan and why is he not being cited here? Then, of course, I realized that you end your book with him, which I enjoyed, particularly because I admire Hassan and his work. I also think that he is under-appreciated not only in Euro-America but also in Egypt. Did you know Ihab Hassan personally? What can you tell us about him? And why should everyone read him?

MW: I never met Ihab Hassan. I think there was no interest. The reason for this can be attributed to his essay *The Question of Postmodernism*, wherein he recognizes that this term is ambiguous and particular to Western civilization. Then he rejects defining it under the pretext that doing so would fix the term, and he is against fixity. Thus, how can these ideas be influential?

RB: Since you are an expert on Ibn Rushd, it is fair to ask you: Would you tell readers why it is vital for them to familiarize themselves with the work of Ibn Rushd?

MW: Ibn Rushd's thinking must become widespread, among the readership in the Islamic world, since he is the only one capable of displacing Ibn Taymiyyah's thought, which is the foundation of Wahhabism and the Muslim Brotherhood. Ibn Taymiyyah is the one who eliminated Ibn Rushd from the Islamic world because Ibn Rushd was for reasoning when it comes to the religious text.

References

Asad, T., Brown, W., Butler, J., & Mahmood, S. (2009). *Is critique secular?: Blasphemy, injury, and free speech*. Berkeley, CA: The Regents of the University of California.

Braidotti, R. (2008). In spite of the times. *Theory, Culture & Society, 25*(6), 1–24. doi:10.1177/0263276408095542

Curtis, A. (Director). (2004). *The power of nightmares: The rise of the politics of fear* [Motion picture]. UK: BBC.

Fadl, K. A. (2005). *The great theft: Wrestling Islam from the extremists*. New York, NY: HarperCollins.

Hassan, I. (1981). The question of postmodernism. *Performing Arts Journal, 6*(1), 30–37. doi:10.2307/3245219

Huntington, S. P. (1996). *The clash of civilizations and the remaking of world order*. New York, NY: Simon & Schuster.

Said, E. W. (1983). *The world, the text, and the critic*. Cambridge, MA: Harvard University Press.

Wahba, M. (1995). *Fundamentalism and secularization*. Cairo, Egypt: Dar Al-Thaqafa.

TRANSLATOR'S PREFACE TO THE ENGLISH EDITION

Dr. Mourad Wahba is Emeritus Professor of Philosophy at Ain Shams University. He is the author of more than twenty books on philosophy and politics, and the coeditor, with Mona Abousenna, of *Averroës and the Enlightenment* (Wahba & Abousenna, 1996). Finally, he is the founder of the Afro-Asian Philosophy Association.

Although Wahba is an Egyptian philosopher, he is really a *world philosopher* in the truest sense of the phrase since he synthesizes Euro-American and Afro-Asian philosophies in both of his thinking and writing. In *Fundamentalism and Secularization*, Wahba (1995) traces the philosophical and political origins of fundamentalism and secularization as praxes in an effort to theorize their antithetical relationship throughout history, and how that antagonism is affected by the dialectics of global capitalism and, more recently, postmodernism. I agree with most, if not all, of Wahba's arguments in the book, but I must add a number of caveats, which are also reflected in my preceding interview with Professor Wahba.

(1) Is "fundamentalism" the best term for explaining the phenomenon of terrorism in the twentieth and twenty-first centuries (cf. Abou El Fadl, 2005)? If so, how can we make sure that States do not abuse this term to their own advantage? Expressed in a different way, how can we prevent States that claim to be fighting fundamentalists from using this claim as an excuse to oppress dissenting citizens?

This question leads to my next point, which concerns the principal intervention against fundamentalism. (2) Secularization is neither a dogma nor an ideology; if anything, it is, as an imperfect process, a critical attitude vis-à-vis the theologization of politics. In other words, secularization, or de-dogmatization, is *not* concerned with religious peoples, for, as a rule, democratic republics must guarantee their citizens and residents, especially minorities, the right to freely practice any or no religion. In that sense, secularization can neither be a violent intervention nor a fixed ideology like secularism or *Laïcité*, as is the case in France. This is why I regard Edward Said's notions of "secular criticism" (1983) and "democratic criticism" (2004) to be crucial safeguards for realizing the process of secularization. (3) Like Wahba, I am equally critical of postmodernism and I am not for the wholesale rejection of the Enlightenment either. However, I also believe that we should not overlook the critical modernists' analysis of modernity, such as the Frankfurt School's critique of the Enlightenment as "totalitarian" (Adorno & Horkheimer, 1944/1997, p. 6) or Zygmunt Bauman's (1989) argument, "It was the *rational* world of *modern* civilization that made the Holocaust thinkable" (p. 13, emphasis added). (4) For this reason, I find Enrique Dussel's (2013) decolonial concept of *transmodernity* to be quite helpful here, for it actually names a third (wordly) attitude vis-à-vis modernity, which I believe is embodied by Wahba's approach in the book—although, to be fair, he does not agree with me regarding this characterization.

Transmodernity describes an inclusive, or pluriversal, vision of the world from the perspective of the oppressed, particularly in the Global South. Hence, transmodernity is not a rejection of modernity but, rather, an affirmation of both modernity and its alterity, which entails the worlding of philosophy and history among other fields of knowledge. This affirmation, and this worlding, certainly entails delinking modernity from coloniality. As such, while bearing the distinction between *secularism as a Eurocentric ideology* and *secularization as a worldcentric process* in mind, my attempt has been to practice what Lena Salaymeh (2021) calls "decolonial translation" as "a tool for disrupting the epistemic hegemony of coloniality" (p. 16), which she contrasts with colonial forms of non-translation, partial translation, and/or mistranslation from Arabic to English vis-à-vis the Islamic tradition in the context of what she terms the "coloniality trinity" of "secularism, state, law" (p. 17).

Although the book was originally published in 1995, it is extremely relevant now more than ever given the current state of world affairs: the specters of religious terrorism, parasitic capitalism, and humanitarian imperialism—not mentioning authoritarianism and fascism. In the book, Wahba posits a number of original theoretical claims, but his central argument concerns the organic, or dialectical, relationship between religious fundamentalisms and parasitic capitalism, on the one hand, and postmodernism, on the other hand. Wahba is equally critical of religious fundamentalisms and parasitic capitalism, which for him are obstructions to secularization and democracy. In this sense, I read him as a Radical Leftist (as opposed to Liberal Centrist or Conservative Rightist), which speaks to his worldcentric vision vis-à-vis secularization as a process.

In other words, I do not think Wahba is inherently against non-secular traditions (e.g., Islam) or has an issue with what Talal Asad (2018) calls "ritualization" (p. 25). Wahba's triple critique is directed equally at: (1) fundamentalists *qua* dogmatists, who claim to be "the bearers of the Absolute Truth," to use his language, (2) parasitic capitalists, and (3) postmodernists. Therefore, his worldcentric use of secularization performs a dialectical ideology critique and does not embody a "Eurocentric ideology" (Salaymeh, 2020). For example, Wahba approaches the Islamic tradition on its own terms without viewing it through the lens of European Christianity, of which he is equally critical as is clear from his argument that Edmund Burke is the key theorist of fundamentalism.

My aim with translating this book from Arabic to English is to introduce English-speaking students and scholars to an overlooked but noteworthy politico-philosophical take on salient topics by an author who fares from North Africa. I think it is crucial, particularly for those living in the Global North, to consider these topics from the perspective of the Global South in order to compare and contrast how the dynamics of religious fundamentalisms manifest themselves in different cultural contexts around the world.

The scope of the book (or Part I) is large, for, in Chapters 1 and 2, Wahba theorizes fundamentalism and secularization as historical ideas before treating them philosophically as political practices. In Chapter 3, Wahba focuses on North Africa and West Asia (NAWA) as a case study to demonstrate the antithetical relationship between fundamentalism and secularization, and how the failure of the latter contributes to the success of the former. In Chapter 4, Wahba explores the theoretical terrain of postmodernism in an effort to investigate its exacerbation of the fundamentalism-capitalism dialectic. His critique goes to show that religions or traditions are not to be solely blamed for the rise of fundamentalisms during the Cold War and beyond.

In Chapter 1, Wahba performs an archeology/genealogy of fundamentalism tracing the concept back to Edmund Burke, whose ideas he considers to be at the root of the contemporary Conservative Christian movement. This archeology/genealogy helps the reader conceptualize the philosophical foundation for two different but related fundamentalist groups today: Christian and Muslim fundamentalists. While these two groups certainly have their differences, they are both essentially a manifestation of a reactionary Conservative movement—two sides of the same ideological coin. Fundamentalists are neither reformists like the Liberal Centrists nor revolutionaries like the Radical Leftists. The Radical Left, in Wahba's and my opinion, possess the antidote to religious fundamentalisms in the form of a revolutionary socialist program grounded in both secular humanism and radical democracy. The Liberal Centrists are somewhat responsible, along with the Conservative Right, for the rise of religious fundamentalisms, in the twentieth and twenty-first centuries, with their embrace of what Wahba (1995) labels "parasitic capitalism," which I understand to mean neoliberalism, but parasitism can also be framed in terms of imperialism as the highest stage of capitalism (Lenin, 1917/2017).

For Wahba (1995), parasitic capitalism "devours what is against science and reason, that is, everything that leads to absent-mindedness," hence, its dialectical relationship with religious fundamentalism as a praxis of literalism, which is inherently antagonistic to interpretation. Interestingly, in my interview with Wahba, he mentions, "terrorism is the highest stage of religious fundamentalisms." If we stretch Lenin's and Wahba's logics regarding capitalism and fundamentalism, then I would argue that there is also a dialectical, or organic, relationship between imperialism and terrorism.

Wahba's dialectical method vis-à-vis fundamentalism can be characterized as a form of immanent critique since he deconstructs fundamentalisms from within their own logics; for example, Islamic fundamentalism in particular is analyzed through the lens of a Muslim rationalist like Ibn Rushd. Wahba, however, does not single out Islam or Muslims as inherently flawed like an Islamophobic Orientalist would; instead, he writes, "Islam, in terms of being a tolerant religion, par excellence, is biased toward peaceful coexistence with other religions." The problem of fundamentalism, for him, is not specific to Islam—for example, "I say fundamentalism without mentioning the Islamic sign because this is fundamentalism whatever its religious sign may be"—and he, in fact, shows that fundamentalism can manifest in relation to the Abrahamic faiths as a whole and even beyond. Paul Virilio, for instance, speaks of "technological fundamentalism" as "the religion of those who believe in the absolute power of technology" (as cited in Armitage, 1999, p. 44). Like Wahba, Virilio rejects most absolutes, which for him are essentially totalitarian. As an antitotalitarian, Virilio is in favor of "fractalization" (p. 33) on the basis of Einstein's theory of relativity. However, for Virilio—as a function of his anarcho-Christianity—there is an exception, an absolute he believes in: "You cannot deconstruct the absolute necessity of justice" (p. 39). Is secularization functioning as an absolute then for Wahba one might ask? No, as a politico-epistemological process, secularization asks relative, or worldly, questions as opposed to providing absolute answers grounded in theological treatments that literalize the sacred.

Fundamentalism then, for Wahba, is a function of a literalist attitude vis-à-vis tradition. In other words, as a claim for the Absolute Truth, fundamentalism is the negation of interpretation. And secularization, he argues, is not an ideological panacea like secularism or *laïcité*, but the very process of, or condition for, democratic interpretation, which is always relative. In fact, Wahba (1995) regards secularization as "a theory of knowledge," "the passage to rationalism," and a "transfer of power"; he defines it as follows: "thinking of what is relative in relative terms and not in absolute terms." The conditions for fundamentalism, Wahba argues, are parasitic capitalism and postmodernism, which constitute a fertile ground for the bearers of the Absolute Truth, who are against both socialism and interpretation, respectively.

Here I must add that I characterize Wahba as an epistemic relativist as opposed to a moral relativist because he clearly has specific values, such as his belief that nothing is beyond interpretation—hence, his epistemic relativism. Wahba basically believes that human subjects should be able to critically think, write, and talk about any object of knowledge including, and maybe especially, taboo topics.

One of Wahba's main themes in the book is that the ideological core of all religious fundamentalisms is more or less the same. This argument is similar to the links that Adam Curtis (2004) makes in his documentary film *The Power of Nightmares: The Rise of the Politics of Fear*. In the film, Curtis juxtaposes American neoconservatism to militant Islamism, in the context of the Soviet-Afghan War, to show the ideological resemblance between these two warring factions. This resemblance between neoconservatism and Islamism is a residue of the United States' material support, during the Arab Cold War (1952–79), for a number of Persian Gulf monarchies, which in turn employed Wahhabism in their ideological fight against Arab socialism, particularly its leader Gamal Abdel Nasser. Having said that, it is worth reiterating that Wahba's book was published six years before the tragic events of 9/11 and the ensuing, and ongoing, global "war on terror." Consequently, it is fair to assert that this book is ahead of its time.

Furthermore, Wahba not only shows us that there is an organic, or dialectical, relationship between fundamentalisms and capitalism/postmodernism. He also provides us, in Chapter 2, with the necessary tools (e.g., secularization) for critically thinking about the world today, particularly in the context of the ceaseless rise of reactionary movements, Statist or otherwise. *Fundamentalism and Secularization* demonstrates that the Alt-Right did not appear out of nowhere. They are a continuation of the New Right or the Moral Majority movement spearheaded by Jerry Falwell. In addition to Wahba's extraordinarily accurate prognostic and diagnostic vision, he presents his readers with conceptual tools from the archives of world philosophy. Wahba's world philosophical approach is compelling because he is an erudite scholar, who was trained in both Euro-American and Afro-Asian philosophies. This type of intercultural dialogue that he embodies, through not only his knowledge but also his being, is exactly what we need to see more of today. In this vein, Wahba (2006) strongly suggests Ibn Rushd as a bridge between the Global North and the Global South.

My task, as a translator, consisted of sticking as closely as possible to both Wahba's logic and rhetoric. However, the structural differences between Arabic and English as languages from two disparate families—Semitic and West Germanic, respectively—

necessitated some flexibility on my part in order for the text's original light to shine through more fully, particularly in instances of cultural difference. For example, the Arabic concept of *dawla*, which can mean dynasty or cycle, predates the nation-state and is closer to the ancient Greek idea of *kyklos* (i.e., cyclical change). Wael Hallaq (2012) captures the impermanence of *dawla* when he writes, "Thus the Community [*Ummah*] remains fixed and cannot come to an end until the Day of Judgment, whereas the *dawla* that governs it is temporary and ephemeral, having no intrinsic, organic, or permanent ties to the Community and its Sharī'a" (p. 63, emphasis in original). For this reason, I have opted to translate *al-dawlah al-Islāmīyah* as Islamic governance (*al-hukm al-Islami*) as opposed to the Islamic state to bracket unnecessary associations with the infamous terrorist organization (i.e., ISIL). Also, some terms (e.g., *al-sunnah*), I define in more than way because the word's complexity in Arabic cannot really be rendered using a single word in English. Such polysemous terms I translate while including their transliterations in brackets or vice versa.

Furthermore, the Arabic word *al-hadatha* can signify modernity (as an era), modernism (as a movement), or modernization (as a process); for the most part, Wahba is referring to modernism, but in some cases he is indexing modernity. I tried to discern this difference based on the context in which the word appears—for example, whether the context is a literary aesthetic (e.g., Sontag's), particularly when contrasted with postmodernism, or a certain historical period that began roughly in the fifteenth century and which came to fruition with the Enlightenment in the seventeenth century.

The aforementioned flexibility, or "freedom of linguistic flux" (Benjamin, 1923/1996, p. 261), speaks to when literal translation—that is, "fidelity to the word" or "reproduction of meaning" (p. 259)—becomes real translation, that is, "transparent" (p. 260); after all, the task of the translator entails, as Walter Benjamin (1923/1996) reminds us, "finding the particular intention toward the target language which produces in that language the echo of the original" (p. 258). For Benjamin (1923/1996), translation, as a form, issues from the afterlife of an original text (p. 254); Derrida (2001), similarly, indexes the macabre when he characterizes translation as "a travail of mourning" (p. 199). In other words, translating is not cloning. Translation is akin to reincarnation. The body of the original text dies in the process, but the text's soul remains eternal through "reverberation" (Benjamin, 1923/1996, p. 258). This eternal—or perhaps spiritual—dimension, that is, the "translatability" (p. 254) of a text, is what Benjamin (1923/1996) means by "pure language" (p. 257).

Additionally, Wahba's pluriversal vision as a world philosopher who believes "though it contains many diverse cultures, human civilization is one" (Wahba & Abousenna, 2010, p. 24) made the task of translating his book enjoyable, for he is not writing from the perspective of the false "clash of civilizations" hypothesis (Huntington, 1993). Wahba (1995), in fact, refers instead to "the clash of the Absolutes" as a clash between the fundamentalists of the world (cf. Ali, 2002), who clearly do not believe in a single human civilization and who may actually be committed to the destruction of said civilization—an antihumanist impulse that Wahba characterizes as "Tatarian."

In translating Wahba's masterpiece from Arabic to English, I maintained close fidelity to the spirit of the original text. I also went through Wahba's references, which was a fascinating, albeit arduous, research process. All of my notes, or edits, as a translator are included in brackets [like this]. Sometimes, I have opted to not translate certain Arabic words, but rather to transliterate them or Romanize them, particularly when I found that a certain concept in Arabic (e.g., *Allāh*) has no real equivalence in English—God is a generic term but not the specific name of the deity worshiped in the Islamic tradition. Often times, I have included both the translation and the transliteration through the use of brackets. Further, Professor Wahba and I came to an agreement around my use of gender-neutral language (e.g., the human instead of man) throughout the English translation with two exceptions: (1) unless there is a direct reference cited in the text, which employs gendered language or (2) the use of He/Him/His as gender pronouns to refer to *Allāh*. This is a linguistic convention in Arabic, so while *Allāh* is not *naturally* masculine (for He transcends gender), He is *grammatically* masculine.

In addition to Part I of this book, which is my translation of *Fundamentalism and Secularization*, we managed to secure copyright clearances from Wiley in order to include, in Part II, two previously published essays by Professor Wahba: *The Concept of the Good in Islamic Philosophy* (1997) and *Philosophy in North Africa* (2004). These two essays certainly complement some of the themes explored in *Fundamentalism and Secularization*.

In sum, Wahba's foundational ethic is: one civilization, many cultures. This secular humanist ethic is, of course, the complete opposite of the propagandistic and reactionary "clash of civilizations" ideology, which is an imperialist logic sustaining many of the endless wars we continue to bear witness to today. This book, which can be rendered as a material praxis of ideology critique, is intended for students and scholars who are interested in world philosophy and history, critical theory, and geopolitics in general as well as those who are interested in the NAWA region or the topics of fundamentalism and secularization in particular.

References

Abou El Fadl, K. M. (2005). *The great theft: Wrestling Islam from the extremists*. New York, NY: HarperCollins.

Adorno, T. W., & Horkheimer, M. (1944/1997). *Dialectic of enlightenment* (J. Cumming, Trans.). New York, NY: Verso.

Ali, T. (2002). *The clash of fundamentalisms: Crusades, jihads and modernity*. Verso.

Armitage, J. (1999). From modernism to hypermodernism and beyond: An interview with Paul Virilio. *Theory, Culture & Society*, 16(5–6), 25–55.

Asad, T. (2018). *Secular translations: Nation-state, modern self, and calculative reason*. Columbia University Press.

Bauman, Z. (1989). *Modernity and the Holocaust*. Polity Press.

Benjamin, W. (1996). The task of the translator. In M. Bullock & M. W. Jennings (eds.), *Walter Benjamin: Selected writings, volume 1, 1913–1926* (pp. 253–63). Harvard University Press.

Curtis, A. (Director). (2004). *The power of nightmares: The rise of the politics of fear* [Motion picture]. UK: BBC.

Derrida, J. (2001). What is a "relevant" translation?. *Critical Inquiry*, 27(2), 174–200.

Dussel, E. (2013). *Ethics of liberation: In the age of globalization and exclusion* (E. Mendieta, C. P. Bustillo, Y. Angulo, & N. Maldonado-Torres, Trans.). Durham, NC: Duke University Press.

Hallaq, W. B. (2012). *The impossible state: Islam, politics, and modernity's moral predicament*. Columbia University Press.

Huntington, S. (1993). The clash of civilizations. *Foreign Affairs*, 72(3), 22–49.

Lenin, V. I. (1917/2017). Imperialism: The highest stage of capitalism. In P. Gasper (Ed.), *Imperialism and war: Classic writings by V. I. Lenin and Nikolai Bukharin*. Haymarket.

Said, E. W. (1983). Secular criticism. In *The world, the text, and the critic*. Cambridge, MA: Harvard University Press.

Salaymeh, L. (2020, September 14). The eurocentrism of secularism. Universität Erfurt. https://www.uni-erfurt.de/philosophische-fakultaet/forschung/forschungsgruppen/was-ist-westlich-am-westen/west-windows/26-the-eurocentrism-of-secularism.

Salaymeh, L. (2021). Decolonial translation: Destabilizing coloniality in secular translations of Islamic law. *Journal of Islamic Ethics*, 5, 1–28. doi: https://doi.org/10.1163/24685542-12340054

Wahba, M. (1995). *Fundamentalism and secularization*. Cairo, Egypt: Dar Al-Thaqafa.

Wahba, M. (1997). The concept of the good in Islamic philosophy. In E. Deutsch & R. Bontekoe (eds.), *A companion to world philosophies* (pp. 484–92). Wiley-Blackwell.

Wahba, M. (2004). Philosophy in North Africa. In K. Wiredu (ed.), *A Companion to African Philosophy* (pp. 161–171). Wiley-Blackwell.

Wahba, M. (2006). Averroes as a bridge. *Think*, 4(12), 13–16.

Wahba, M., & Abousenna, M. (Eds.). (1996). *Averroës and the Enlightenment*. Amherst, NY: Prometheus Books.

Wahba, M., & Abousenna, M. (2010, June/July). Why secularization failed in the Muslim world. *Free Inquiry*, 30(4), 23–6.

AUTHOR'S PREFACE TO THE ARABIC EDITION (1995)

This is the first book in the *Issues of the Day* series, and it is titled *Fundamentalism and Secularization*. I think fundamentalism comes first because, to be precise, it is the issue of the day. The violence, terrorism, killing, and illegal economic activities that humanity is currently suffering from are but branches of fundamentalism in its organic relationship with parasitic capitalism.

I have been occupied with researching this issue since its emergence in the 1970s to discover that its root extends back to 1790, the year in which Edmund Burke's book *Reflections on the Revolution in France* was released. This book is the constitution of religious fundamentalisms with their differing nomenclature, for Burke characterizes the Enlightenment in terms of barbarity and ignorance.

If the Enlightenment is characteristically secular, then fundamentalism is the negation of secularization. This stated antagonism between fundamentalism and secularization is the book's central idea.

PART I

FUNDAMENTALISM AND SECULARIZATION

1

What Is Fundamentalism?

What is the role of religion in today's world? Or, more precisely: What roles do the eleven[1] [largest and medium-sized] religions play in today's world?

The answer to this question warrants, to begin with, determining the features of today's world. What are these features?

The path of today's world is governed by tomorrow's world because tomorrow is the future and the starting point since history moves from the future and not from the past. What is this history?

There are terms that are starting to become prevalent now that could define the features of a futuristic vision; they are "universalism," "globalism," "and interdependence."

Universalism is a style of thinking that is trying to holistically understand the universe or more precisely, reality—returning the parts to this whole. A universal vision establishes itself by rejecting closure and remaining open and self-critical, its purpose being establishing a universal consciousness that obliterates human alienation in this universe. Religions, in all their varieties, have put forth universal visions. And now, thanks to the scientific and technological revolution, space has been invaded, and it is now possible for science to present a scientific, universal vision.

As for globalism, it arises from universalism, and it means viewing planet Earth as a singularity and not as assembled from independent parts.

That is why interdependence is necessary in globalism, for it is the negation of both dependence and the traditional understanding of independence, that is, the negation of the absolute authority of the State; therefore, it is impossible to solve regional problems, such as overpopulation, environmental pollution, and the crisis of natural resources, except within a framework of globalism. However, interdependence is no longer restricted to regional problems but extends to scientific problems, as science can no longer function in isolation from the other sciences. The emergence of "interdisciplinary sciences" forms a bridge between the different sciences, wherein it is possible, in the end, to realize the unity of knowledge within a framework of the universe's unity.

The realization of this unity elicits a questioning of the destiny of this abundance of religions, or, more precisely, it provokes an inquiry into the relationship between the one and the many. Religious philosophies have faced this query, but in the scope of the relationship between God and the world, their question was: How do the many emanate from the one? Although there are multiple answers, they could be reduced to two answers.

One of them is occupied with the unity of existence, so does not distinguish between the one and the many. Perhaps the Indians were the first people to express this doctrine, wherein all that exists emanates from Brahma as a general source. Will, in Brahma, is about the desire of abundance and uniqueness. As for natural philosophers, in sixth-century BCE Greece, they had reduced all that exists, as a whole, to one substance that varied according to their various opinions: water for Thales, air for Anaximenes, and fire for Heraclitus.

Emanationism was the other answer; Plotinus was taken by this theory, and it relates that one is a simplex to the extent that one negates Rationalizing and Understanding. So if something flows, it flows from the one oriented toward themself. In this orientation to themself, they see and their vision contemplates their Logos. As their Logos contemplates things that are at their disposal, it gives birth to the Universal Soul. And from this multitude, Number, Quantity, and Quality are born. Ibn Sīnā [Avicenna] and al-Fārābī [Alpharabius] were influenced by the theory of emanation, which led to their creation of the theory of ten intellects.

That was long ago. As for now, the question of the relationship between the one and the many is not presented within the framework of the question of creation but of world peace.

The question then becomes: What is the relationship between world peace and this abundance of religions? To answer this question requires an inquiry into every religion's view of the other religions in the modern era. In 1860, the first conference on missions was held in Liverpool with a research focus on non-Christian religions because of the political hegemony of Christian culture. What is noteworthy is that three years before the conference was held, a number of missionaries were killed amid the violence of the Indian Mutiny of 1857. Eleven years after the conference, Bishop John Coleridge Patteson was killed in Melanesia. Additionally, a hundred missionaries were killed in

China. As the nineteenth century came to a close, missionaries were living in isolation. And in 1871, Edward Burnett Tylor published his two-volume book, *Primitive Culture*. On the first page of the first section, which is titled *The Science of Culture*, he says:

> The condition of culture among the various societies of mankind [*sic*], in so far as it is capable of being investigated on general principles, is a subject apt for the study of laws of human thought and action. On the one hand, the uniformity which so largely pervades civilization may be ascribed, in great measure, to the uniform action of uniform causes; while on the other hand its various grades may be regarded as stages of development or evolution, each the outcome of previous history, and about to do its proper part in shaping the history of the future. [Tylor, 1871/2016, p. 25][2]

Tylor then unveiled the existence of non-Christian religious ideas among peoples that were regarded [by Europeans] as barbarians.

In 1875, Max Müller published the first book in the series, *The Sacred Books of the East*, wherein he tackled the religions of Asia. And in 1890, Frazer published his book, *The Golden Bough*, which was received with astonishment and appreciation. The reason for this is his demonstration that Christianity is not the only religion. In 1965, Pope John XXIII called for the Second Vatican Council and ended up with recommendations—among which was the establishment of *Nostra Aetate: Declaration of the Church to Non-Christian Religions*—given that God unveiled themself in new forms of faith. And in 1968, the Temple of Understanding's first Spiritual Summit Conference was held in Calcutta, India, and it included representatives from the eleven religions. The theme of the conference was the significance of religion in the modern world. All of the research generated during the conference revolved around the finding that no religion holds the Absolute Truth, but each religion holds a form of the truth. Therefore, there is no justification for any religion's superiority over another, and the negation of this justification entails proving another justification, which is the necessity for the convergence of the various religious forms of truth since they can be considered perspectives on an Absolute Truth. Subsequently, no religion has the right to determine this Absolute Truth because any religion's determination of this truth involves the omission of the other religions. So if a faith claims that *religion is the belief in God and eternity*, then this saying signifies omitting Confucianism since it does not hold that belief. And if a faith is determined by revelation, there are religions free of revelation. Certainly, the phrase "the Absolute Truth" arouses our questioning about its origin and the justification for bearing it.

Philosophically, it can be said that the human, since their inception, sought the Absolute Truth by virtue of the human mind's propensity for the unification of human knowledge. It is for this reason that they wander through every field of this knowledge. Then, in an organic unity, they join all the fields together, and link them, which prevents the separation of a part from the whole since that may lead to the Being's complete elimination. The propensity of the mind for oneness is, at the same time, a propensity for the Absolute.[3] The human seeks the Absolute Truth as well by virtue of feeling unsettled in this unknown universe.

However, attaining the Absolute Truth was never a simple matter. As Absolute Truths have multiplied, the Absolute has subsequently multiplied; the Absolute's multiplicity entered into a liminal contradiction by virtue of the Absolute's unity—that it cannot but be one. Accordingly, the human is a bearer of the Absolute Truth, is barred from [by] it, or is searching for it. Furthermore, in Ancient Greece, this trinity crystallized philosophically, and it was in a state of conflict, but the bearers of the Absolute Truth prevailed.

Breaking it down: in the fifth century BCE, Anaxagoras denied the divine nature of the heavenly bodies. He went on to say that the Moon is a land on which there are mountains and valleys, and that the sun and the planets are fiery stones, whose nature is no different from the nature of earthly bodies. The bearers of the Absolute Truth could not stand such a saying, as uttered by Anaxagoras, because they believed that all that is heavenly is divine, and that whoever deals with such things in a scientific manner is committing treason. They accused him of impiety, so he was forced to leave Athens, where he was living and philosophizing.

Then Protagoras came to Athens around 450 BCE, and he published a book titled *Truth*, wherein the following phrase appeared: "The human is the measure of all things." The meaning of this phrase is that the truth is relative to the human's relativity. Subsequently, out of this phrase, he constructed another phrase, which is his saying: "I cannot know whether the gods exist or do not exist. Many things stand in the way between me and this knowledge, especially the ambiguity of the matter and the shortness of life." Thus, Protagoras was accused of impiety and his books were burned, and he was sentenced the death penalty, but he ran away.

As for Socrates, he believed that his wisdom arose from his knowledge of his own ignorance [simple ignorance] as opposed to others who were ignorant but pretended to know [double ignorance]. No sooner had he gone on to dialogue with politicians on extensive occasions than it was brought to light to them that they knew nothing, so they accused him of impiety and corruption of the youth. He was sentenced the death penalty, a verdict which Socrates accepted.

In the last half of the second century CE, a sect of skeptics originated under the leadership of Sextus Empiricus, that is, the experimental Sextus. It transpires in one of his writings that the basic principle for the doctrine of skepticism, around which it revolves, is: "For every argument there is a counterargument." He then goes on to say: "We believe that of the prerequisites for this principle is the arrival at a point, at which we cease to be dogmatic." And the meaning of this, according to him, is that "the skeptic refuses dogma."[4] What is peculiar, in the case of Sextus and his companions, is that the translation of their writings is both rare and difficult to find. Our ignorance of the texts of this school of skepticism resulted in the word "skeptic" being emptied out of its meaning. Our ignorance of the texts is, most likely, a function of the authority of the bearers of the Absolute Truth, that is, the dogmatists.

In twelfth-century Córdoba, Ibn Rushd [Averroës] called for the philosopher's right in "interpreting" religious texts consistent with intellectual reasoning. Ibn Rushd defined interpretation as "extension of the significance of an expression from real to metaphorical significance" [Ibn Rushd, 1179/2012, p. 50]. He made that statement concerning the relationship between Divine Law [sharī'ah] and intellectual reasoning. According to him:

This being so, whenever demonstrative study leads to any manner of knowledge about any being, that being is inevitably either unmentioned or mentioned in Scripture. If it is unmentioned there is no contradiction, and it is in the same case an act whose category is unmentioned, so that the lawyer has to infer it by reasoning from Scripture. If Scripture speaks about it, the apparent meaning of the words inevitably either accords or conflicts with the conclusions of demonstration about it. If this . . . accords there is no argument. If it conflicts there is a call for allegorical interpretation. [Ibn Rushd, 1179/2012, p. 50][5]

Interpretation is about breaking consensus [*ijmāʿ*] because "there has never been a consensus [against allegorical interpretation]," according to Ibn Rushd [p. 53],[6] and this prevents accusing the interpreter of apostasy [*takfīr*]. And for this reason, Ibn Rushd criticized al-Ghazzālī [Algazelus] when the latter accused Muslim philosophers, such as al-Fārābī and Ibn Sīnā, of apostasy. Nevertheless, Ibn Rushd was accused of apostasy and his writings were burned; his sentence was to be exiled in the town of Lucena [al-Yussana].

In the seventeenth century, Galileo declared his partiality for Copernican theory, which centered on the largest celestial body (the sun) remaining motionless; meanwhile, the smaller celestial bodies revolved around it, which is a greater realization of the principle of parsimony than the revolution of all celestial bodies around the Earth. Galileo was accused of heresy because of his partiality for a theory, which negates the Holy Book, and he was tried before an inquisition tribunal or, more precisely, before the bearers of the Absolute Truth.

Also, in the seventeenth century, *A Letter Concerning Toleration* was anonymously published. Its author was the English philosopher John Locke. In the beginning of the *Letter*, Locke denounces Enthusiasts[7] and this English term is synonymous to the term "Fanatics."[8] These terms were marginal in the sixteenth century, but then they became central in philosophical and theological debates. Whatever the case may be, it is worth noting that toleration, for Locke, is based on an epistemological theory, which is concerned with the limits of the human mind, and he concludes from this that religious tenets can neither be confirmed nor disconfirmed. Therefore, the human either believes in them or not, which is why it is not possible for one to impose them on another. Thus, Locke refuses the principle of persecution in the name of religion. Refusing this principle is a prerequisite for the obligation of toleration—hence, Locke's distinction between the civil government and matters of religion. In my estimation, this distinction or separation is an effect of secularization and not a cause for secularization—as secularization is a theory of knowledge, and not a political theory, because secularization, according to my definition, is "thinking of what is relative in relative terms and not in absolute terms."

In the eighteenth century, Enlightenment philosophy was spreading. It crystallized in Kant's philosophy, wherein the mind was unable to grasp the Absolute. Kant, in the preface to the first edition of his book *Critique of Pure Reason*, says:

> Human reason has the peculiar fate in one species of its cognitions that it is burdened with questions which it cannot dismiss, since they are given to it as problems by the nature of reason itself, but which it also cannot answer, since they transcend every capacity of human reason. [Kant, 1781/1998, p. 99]

These questions revolve around the concept of the Absolute whether we call it by the word "God" or the "State." The story of philosophy, in

Kant's opinion, is not only the story of this inability to answer these questions but also the story of an illusion, which holds the human captive once they imagine the possibility of incontrovertibly grasping the Absolute. However, once grasped the Absolute becomes relative.

From here, Kant distinguishes between two conditions: the condition of searching for a grasp of the Absolute and the condition of grasping the Absolute. In reality, there are many attempts at searching for a grasp of the Absolute. But the human, who imagines that they have incontrovertibly grasped the Absolute, descends into dogmatism. This is the significance of Kant's saying: "I freely admit that the remembrance of *David Hume* was the very thing that many years ago first interrupted my dogmatic slumber" [Kant, 1783/2004, p. 10, emphasis in original]. And here it is imperative to raise two questions:

What is dogmatism?

And what is the relationship between dogmatism and the Absolute Truth?

Dogma is originally Greek, it means the rule or the principle, and it does not mean the truth. But it was used, later on, to express the decisions of the Christian assemblies vis-à-vis the Absolute Truth, which mandated that they who deny the Absolute Truth be accused of apostasy and heresy. So was the case in Islam, hence the emergence of Islamic scholasticism [*'ilm al-kalām* or the science of discourse]. If Islamic scholasticism was called the science of oneness [*ilm al-tawḥīd*], it is because it stands against theology, that is, the theology of Trinity. In order to confirm *Allāh*'s oneness, the apologetic theologians [*mutakallimūn*] went against the heroes of natural forces and causal laws on the premise that *Allāh* is the Primary Mover. And from this angle, the Muʻtazilites accused philosophers of apostasy.[9] The paradox of apostasy, here, is that the Muʻtazilites accused one another of apostasy. Therefore, it can be argued that the Islamic scholasticism is a dogmatic science, that is, a science of the Absolute Truth. Of concern to a dogmatic science are the accompanying cultural taboos, which are forbidden areas of research; as a result, human knowledge ossifies and progress comes to a halt.

This is nowhere evident than in the historical turns, whose characteristic innovations were resisted by dogmatism. In the philosophical turn, during the Ancient Greek era, Socrates was executed for allegedly denying the gods. And in the scientific turn, during the Middle Ages, Galileo was sentenced allegedly for his criticism of religious belief when he sided with Copernican theory. With the multiplicity of Absolute Truths in the other religions' creed sciences [*ʻulūm al-ʻaqāʼid*], religions entered into conflict with one another. The Age of Enlightenment came about exposing the human's descent into the illusion that they are the bearer of the Absolute Truth. The arrival of Kant's critical philosophy articulated the most genuine assessment of this illusion, specifically the function of critical reason in exposing its roots. Consequently, the establishment of a society must not be based upon any particular Absolute, that is, must not be based upon dogma. The antithesis of this proscription is establishing a society through a "social contract." This expression is the title of a book released by Rousseau, in which he asserts that every individual draws up the clauses of the social contract for themselves and for their rights in the society as a whole. Through the clauses of this contract, everyone becomes equal before the law. Thus ends the divine right of the ruler.

The French Revolution broke out adopting the Enlightenment as a foundation for its philosophy. The Enlightenment negates the bearers of the Absolute Truth. However, this negation was never an easy matter. Edmund Burke's book was released, a year after the French Revolution erupted, that is, in 1790; its title was *Reflections on the Revolution in France*. In the book, he claims that liberties are the fruits of inheritance, which get transmitted from the ancestors to the successors without the need to revert liberties to what is called a general right, or a prior right. He also claims that the human cannot look forward to the future without taking a look at what is behind: the ancestors. Furthermore, Burke takes innovation lightly and regards it as the seed of selfishness. As for inheritance, for him, it is the principle of conservatism, as well as the principle of intergenerational communication.[10] Consequently, he is against civic education, which rests on knowing the physical needs of humans and on establishing an enlightened self, who is capable of joining together self-interest and public interest. And this, in Burke's opinion, is nothing but a kind of atheism.[11]

From that perspective, Burke sees that politics should adapt to human nature, and not to the human mind, which is nothing but a product of nature. Therefore, a politician is in need of experience, vision, and instinct, and they do not need to be cold and calculating. Also, it is not possible for humans to reorganize the world because overthrowing the stability of the political system, which civil societies rest on, is a consequence of this reorganization. These civil societies, in turn, are based on a social contract theory differentiated from the one that seventeenth-century philosophers imagined. According to their theory, in the state of nature, which preceded the formation of societies, humans were free; and they gave up a part of their freedom to the State. Burke views that this theory is a myth. The state of nature, for him, was chaotic and primitive. For this reason, the social contract, which involves a permanent and eternal moral force, transpired to remedy this primitive chaos. Humans are committed to moral force before the State and God because the State, and not the will of the people, is the source of political rights. Therefore, the State should be obeyed as long as the State does not deviate from its legitimacy. This means that the purpose of politics, for Burke, is conserving society. And this meaning involves two aspects: the first aspect is protecting the social structure and private property. The second aspect is protecting the existing political system. Such was the case with Britain when it carried out reforms based on the principle of the return to tradition. He says: "We are resolved to keep an established church, an established monarchy, an established aristocracy" [Burke, 1790/1951, p. 88]. Then he notes that these institutions as a whole must be maintained "each in the degree it exists, and in no greater" [Burke, 1790/1951, p. 88]. It may be of necessity sometimes to carry out a reform in a fraction of these institutions but with the goal of maintaining their internal characteristics.

Burke was aware of the diversity of social institutions and their complexities, but he was not aware of their progress. Therefore, it was easy for him to imagine the possibility of reconciling between social institutions through an effective social cohesion. The individual, for him, is not the primary social cell in that, in a hierarchical society, individuals live in groups, and all of these groups have their particular histories, particular rights, and particular identities. A natural aristocracy rules over this society, and it is characterized by its ownership of large swaths of land, its taking pride in tradition, and its enjoyment of leisure time. This economic, social, and political differentiation is the mainstay for both the continuation and the stability of social life.

Furthermore, Burke, like his friend Adam Smith, believes in the profit motive, in free trade, and in the noninterference of the State because this interference would increase wages, and wage increase is conducive to price inflation and loss of profit, therefore, to underproduction and the emergence of unemployment.

Consequently, Burke opposes three radical schools: the rationalism of the Age of Enlightenment, the Romanticism of Rousseau, and the utilitarianism of Bentham. Despite their dissimilarity, these schools share the following ideas:

- That pure reason paves the way for social progress.
- Humans are naturally good, but social institutions have corrupted them.
- Human traditions are deceptive myths.
- Humans have the capacity for infinite progress.
- The moral and political reformer's purpose is freeing humans from ancient creeds and outdated institutions. The future of humanity lies in both a pure freedom and an unlimited democracy. Political power is the instrument of reform.

Burke's opposition goes back to his refusal of the separation between Church and State. They are, in his opinion, one entity because religion is the source of legislation. Thus, no one has the right to change legislation. The source of justice, too, is, through collective wisdom and traditions: the divine system. As such, Burke shook the Age of Enlightenment or the "Age of Ignorance" [Kirk, 1953/2001, p. 110] as he used to call it.

In 1953, Russell Kirk, an American philosopher, released a book titled *The Conservative Mind: From Burke to Eliot*, which is based on Burke's philosophy. Kirk views that divine intent governs society and conscience, that rationality cannot satisfy human needs, and that enjoyment, more than rationality, governs humans. Therefore, both heritage and prejudice are required for preventing humans from responding to the drive of anarchy. "[I]nnovation may be a devouring conflagration, rather than a torch of progress" [Kirk, 1953/2001, p. 69]. The alternative is slow change as it is society's means for self-preservation. Thus, Burke's rivals are rationalists like Enlightenment philosophers, utilitarians like Rousseau, materialists like Marx, or Darwinians. Despite their diversity, the following ideas form a synergy between them:

- The human's susceptibility for realizing wholeness, the limitlessness of social progress, and the human's capacity for holistic development thanks to education, legislation, and environmental change.
- Contempt for heritage, and a disregard for parental wisdom. Taking the mind and materialistic determinism as guides for social leisure.
- A refusal of Burke's description of State personhood as natural, divine, moral, and that it is a spiritual unity "joined in perpetuity by a moral bond among the dead, the living,

and those yet to be born—the community of souls" [Kirk, 1953/2001, p. 72].[12]

- Equity, thus, a critique of property rights—of agricultural property, in particular.

In the 1970s, Burke's and Kirk's ideas were embodied in what was called religious fundamentalism *viz* the eleven religions.

Ergo the question:

What Is Fundamentalism?

The word "fundamentalism" is linguistically derived from *uṣūl* [*fundamentals*]. This term [*al-uṣūliya*] is a translation of the English word "fundamentalism," and it is an evangelical expression derived from another locution, which is *foundation* as in footing. The prophet Isaiah says, "Behold, I lay in Zion for a foundation a stone, a tried stone, a precious corner stone, a sure foundation" [Isaiah 28:16, King James Version].

The editor [Curtis Lee Laws] of the *Watchman Examiner*[13] is the one who, most likely, coined the English term "fundamentalism" in his editorial for the July 1920 issue, wherein he defined fundamentalists as those "who mean to do battle royal for the great fundamentals" [Laws, 1920, as cited in Burggraff, 1995, p. 11]. Also, in all likelihood, a series of booklets, in twelve volumes, published between 1909 and 1915 under the title *The Fundamentals* paved the way for the coinage of this term. Three million copies were freely distributed, which were sent to priests, evangelists, theologians, Sunday schools, and the secretaries of Christian youth organizations.

The ideas raised in these booklets can be classified as follows:

- The fundamentals of faith, such as the truth of hell and the second coming of Christ.
- Attacking the current of Biblical criticism, which revolves around the Bible being an account of religious development.
- Critiquing scientific theories, in particular Darwinism, which rebuts the Genesis creation myth.[14]

These ideas were raised as a reaction against liberal theologians, whose thought centered on two matters:

1. Doubting the Genesis creation myth because of the progress made by the sciences of geology and biology.
2. Regarding original sin, as told in the Book of Genesis, to be just primitive and childish thinking given the non-existence of so-called Adam and Eve.[15]

That being so, the features of fundamentalism crystallized in the beginning of the twentieth century as follows:

1. Acknowledging that there are solutions capable of achieving national victory and of solving social problems, and that any failure attached to any fundamentalist solution can be attributed to the conspiracies of "the wicked" [Psalm 64:2].
2. Acknowledging that political institutions in the capitalist State are part of "the Communist peril" [Hebert, 1957, p. 27]; therefore, "all citizens are indoctrinated" [p. 145].

3. Any renunciation of the fundamental principles is "betraying that Faith" [Hebert, 1957, p. 19].

4. Refusing any interpretation of the religious text.

The ideas of Burke and Kirk crystallized and found their representation in the Christian fundamentalist Moral Majority movement founded in 1979 under the leadership of pastor Jerry Falwell, who considered himself a student of Edmund Burke. This movement claimed to be a moral movement with the contention that political issues, in Falwell's opinion, are moral issues. This movement included 72,000 pastors among four million members.

Falwell announced that he was motivated to establish this movement as a nationalist seeking the consolidation of America's power, that is, through establishing a strong network of defense. Therefore, he called for American military superiority. What drove him to this call is the Nuclear Weapons Council's announcement in 1978 that the Soviet Union had nuclear supremacy over America. This announcement meant that the United States was no longer number one. The reason for this, in the opinion of Falwell and his fellow fundamentalists, is the American liberals' disbelief that the Communists wanted world domination. The fundamentalists [as cited in Viguerie, 1981, p. 112] attest to that through the many sayings that they attribute to the Communists:[16]

> Lenin says: "We stand for permanent revolution."
> And he also says: "As long as capitalism and socialism exist, we cannot live in peace: in the end, one or the other will triumph."

Stalin says: "Can the capitalists be forced out and the roots of capitalism be annihilated without a bitter class struggle? No, it is impossible."

Mao Zedong says: "Every communist must grasp that political power grows out of the barrel of a gun."

Khrushchev says: "I can prophesy that your grandchildren in America will live under socialism."

Brezhnev says: "Our aim is to gain control of the two great houses on which the West depends—the energy treasure of the Persian Gulf and the mineral treasure house of central and southern Africa."

In 1972, during the period when the "SALT I" [Strategic Arms Limitation] talks were taking place, the Soviet Union, under the leadership of Brezhnev-Andropov, released the following decree:

"—to achieve an overwhelming military superiority over the United States, a superiority sufficient to win not only conventional wars in different parts of the world but also an all-out nuclear war;

"—to conceal this superiority from the public with the help of the censorship in the USSR and the pro-Soviet media in the West;

"—to establish Soviet influence in Indochina and Africa with the help of local Communist or pro-Communist forces organized and armed by the Soviet Union;

"—to break the agreement on peace in Vietnam [i.e., the Paris Peace Accords] and the Helsinki agreements" [as cited in Viguerie, 1981, p. 118]

The Christian fundamentalists conclude from this that a Third World War is possible, and that America should take the following actions without hesitation or delay.

Externally

1. Giving up on the politics of peaceful coexistence and adopting the politics of military superiority through a restriction of the export of technology, capital, or loans that may enable the Soviet to strengthen their war industries.

2. Developing the conventional military forces needed for deterring any aggression supported by the Soviet Union.

3. Investing in the diplomatic field, such as recalling the ambassador or cutting ties if the Soviet resorted to using force against its allies, as was the case in relation to the Soviet's invasion of Czechoslovakia in 1968 and Afghanistan in 1979. Freeing America from the issue of arms control because this issue would weaken the United States Armed Forces.

4. Expanding the space of anti-Communist publicity together with supporting Radio Free Europe/Radio Liberty, and stirring unrest inside the Iron Curtain.

Internally

1. Taking interest in the family because its structure is dysfunctional. The ratio of divorce is 1:2, and of illegitimate

children is 1:5. A 1978 statistic showed that illegitimate children outnumber legitimate children in New York. As a result, the Pro-Family Movement was established, and it included Catholics, Protestants, Eastern Orthodox, and Jews. This movement advocated for the necessity of including prayer in public schools and for withholding federal grants from states that refuse to implement this mandate. This movement also urged the boycott of books that undermined women's traditional role in society. The movement's founders perceive that the resistance comes from atheists, socialists, and opportunistic economists who are getting rich thanks to abortion procedures and sex work.[17]

2. Rethinking tax laws. Up to the 1920's, income tax rates (1% - 24%) did not change, but since the election of Roosevelt in 1932, income tax rates have been on the increase. For this reason, Republicans, who are endorsed by fundamentalists, raised the following slogan: "Money in your pocket." The significance of this slogan is to prevent creeping socialism from permeating throughout America. The liberal philosopher Arthur Schlesinger said that there is "no inherent obstacle to the gradual advance of socialism in the United States."[18]

Based upon all of this, Falwell established an alliance between the Moral Majority and Catholics, Jews, and Mormons. With this alliance, he sought "firing theological guns at liberalism, humanism, and secularism" and returning to traditional, conservative values. Also, Falwell was one of the first supporters of the Star Wars project that Reagan called for when he was President.

In 1981, a book titled *The New Right: We're Ready to Lead* was released for Richard Viguerie, one of the leaders of Christian fundamentalism. Falwell wrote the book's introduction,[19] which goes like this:

At this present hour, there can be no questioning the retrogression of America's stability as a free and healthy nation. In the last several years, Americans have literally stood by and watched as godless, spineless leaders have brought our nation floundering to the brink of death.

Too many of our top governmental officials, including judges in high places, legislators, bureaucrats, and politicians, have cared more about getting a vote than about courageously standing for what is right and good for America. Considering that the stability of any group, whether it be a family or a nation, rises and falls upon leadership, it is no wonder that we find America depraved, decadent, and demoralized.

As a parent and as a God-fearing citizen, I respect Mr. Viguerie's courage to speak out regarding liberals and their actions that have significantly occasioned America's perilous condition. Mr. Viguerie speaks with candor. He is blunt and to the point. The vacuum of leadership in America must be filled. Conservative Americans must now take the helm and guide America back to a position of stability and greatness.

Granted that the writer is hardly wholly objective since he himself is one of the key figures in the New Right, nevertheless, I believe that the book provides insight into the thinking of men and women who are leading a movement which, if anything, has been underrated by the news media as to its ultimate impact in American politics.

Mr. Viguerie uses the phrase the New Right[20] to speak of those moral citizens who now must come together and let their voice be heard, those, as he puts it:

- "hard-working citizens sick and tired of high taxes and ever-rising inflation;
- small businessmen angry at excessive governmental regulations and federal red tape;
- born-again Christians disturbed about sex on TV and in movies;
- parents opposed to forced busing;
- supporters of the right to life and against federal financing of abortions;
- middle class Americans tired of Big Government, Big Business, Big Labor and Big Education telling us what to do and what not to do;
- pro-defense citizens alarmed by appeasement and weakness in U.S. foreign policy."

Mr. Viguerie has not detailed a new group; he has described the backbone of our country—those citizens who are pro-family, pro-moral, pro-life, and pro-American, who have integrity and believe in hard work, those who pledge allegiance to the flag and proudly sing our national anthem. He has described that group of citizens who love their country and are willing to sacrifice for her. America was built on faith in God, on integrity, and on hard work. Mr. Viguerie clearly names and points out the actions of those who have not been committed to these principles and have thus led to the weakening and the humiliation of a once great America.

It is now time for moral Americans to band together in a collective voice and make the difference in America by exerting an effort to make their feelings known. The godless minority of treacherous individuals who have been permitted to formulate national policy must now realize they do not represent the majority. They must be made to see that moral Americans are a powerful group who will no longer permit them to destroy our country with their godless, liberal philosophies.

The movement made up of conservative Americans can no longer be ignored and silenced. America's destiny awaits its action. Your children's future welfare will be decided by your present involvement.[21]

This is Christian fundamentalism in the United States in terms of doctrine, party, and rule. A doctrine that dates back to the counter-Enlightenment and its opposition to the French Revolution based on Burke's (1790) *Reflections on the Revolution in France* and Kirk's (1953) *The Conservative Mind*; a party of the Moral Majority under the leadership of pastor Jerry Falwell since 1979; and a rule when Ronald Reagan took over the reins of government in the White House on November 5, 1980. Reagan was elected Governor of California in 1966 with the support of fundamentalists. He was Governor for eight years, during which time the fundamentalists' magazines played an important role in the realization of Reagan's "popularity." Him winning the Presidency was the embodiment of the fundamentalists' dream of taking control of ruling America as a whole.

Christian fundamentalists were prepared to prevent the occurrence of any backlash to this embodiment. Richard Viguerie's [1981] letter to Reagan is proof of this. Here is an excerpt:

Mr. President, I'd like to call to your attention some danger signals I see on the horizon.

You were a good governor of California. That's not just a compliment from me. Most objective political observers agree.

But unfortunately, your achievements didn't last. After you completed your eight years in office, the liberals took over the state's power structures... today it lacks elected leaders devoted to continuing the type of government you gave California.

To be blunt, Mr. President, you apparently gave little thought to building a Conservative/Republican power base in California to help insure that those who shared your views would govern long after you left office.

And I see alarming signs that this pattern is about to be repeated in your presidency... how can you put your principles into effect if most key policy-making positions in your Administration are held by non-conservatives?

I can't overstress the need to include large numbers of the young people who have worked their hearts out for you these last five years. If you fail to do that, many of them will be soured on politics, and a whole generation of potential conservative leaders will be damaged.

America needs a rebirth of religious commitment. I urge you to use your great skills as a communicator and regularly ask people to seek the solution to our personal and national problems in God. [pp. 188–90]

Viguerie [1981] ends his letter saying:

> The New Right, I can assure you, wants to be your friend and strong supporter. . . . We share a common goal with you. We want you to be the best President the U.S. has had in the 20th century. And I firmly believe you can be—simply by being the same man the American people have known, admired, and elected. [p. 191]

This is what Richard Viguerie wrote in 1981. In 1982, President Reagan invited pastor Falwell to visit with him in the White House. In this visit, Reagan promised pastor Falwell to amend the Constitution in order to make prayer obligatory in public schools.

The New Right, or the Radical Right, has been embodied in the last fifty years in three movements: Coughlinism in the 1930s, McCarthyism in the 1950s, and the John Birch Society in the 1960s. There is as much agreement as there is disagreement among these movements.

The agreement centers on them being extremist national movements that are opposed to global liberalism—hence, these movements strive against the basic principles of a democratic society. As for the disagreement, it goes back to the different conditions that led to the emergence of each of these three movements.

Coughlinism is attributed to Father Charles Coughlin. It arose in response to the economic crisis of the 1930s and an international concern for the emergence of fascism, the Spanish Civil War, and the Second World War. Coughlinism was against laissez-faire capitalism as exemplified by the banks and against Jewish influence in the fields of politics and money, but for Franco's anticommunism.

McCarthyism is attributed to Senator McCarthy. It arose in response to a growing communist force inside America, or, more precisely, in response to what McCarthy called "the internal communist threat" that led to China's ruin. McCarthy sharply criticized Eisenhower's politics in the years 1953–4, claiming that they were naïve to ignore the influence of communists on governmental institutions, but he did not direct any criticism at neither the Jews nor ethnic minorities.

As for the John Birch Society, its president was Robert Welch. It arose out of the fundamentalists' centers in Houston, Boston, and Los Angeles, and in response to the Republicans' failure in opposing socialist politics in the United States. Its purpose was combating communism in a communist way.[22]

In addition to these three movements, several anticommunist research circles were established under the leadership of Evangelical pastors. These research circles sought to uncover the secrets of dialectical materialism and to prevent America from sliding toward communism. Their slogan was "no peace with the Soviet" or, more precisely, "the impossibility of peace with the Soviet."

The central idea, then, for the Radical Right, was that communism threatened the United States not only from without but also from within. It is said, as a rebuttal to this idea, that the Communist Party USA is weak, and that its influence on labor unions is almost not worth mentioning. However, there is a counter-rebuttal to this saying from the Radical Right. In their opinion, if this is so then how were Cuba, Czechoslovakia, and China lost? Also, according to them, the Democratic Party leaders are members of "the Communist conspiracy."

The Radical Right were exaggerated in their hostility to communism to the extent that their magazines refrained, for a period of time, to point to the USSR's launching of Sputnik to the Moon as well as their sending of a Soviet human to space.

So it is clear that Christian fundamentalism, in the United States, criticizes liberal society in order to establish a society based on an Absolute, the Christian Absolute. For this reason, it unquestionably extends its criticism to modern science.

In the opinion of Christian fundamentalism, modern science, as exemplified by the theory of evolution, is a pseudoscience because it undermines the Bible's authority. If God did not create the world in six days then the Book of Genesis is invalid, and if one book is false then the Old Testament canon, in its entirety, is invalid.

The modern city, also in the opinion of Christian fundamentalism, produced bureaucracy, which weakens human communication. For this reason, the modern city is against religion, whose function is strengthening human relations. As such, the motto of Christian fundamentalism is: "God created the village, and humans made the city" [cf. Cowper, 1785].

This is Christian fundamentalism, what about Islamic fundamentalism?

In order to define it, I selected three of its greatest thinkers, and they are Abul A'la Maududi, Sayyid Qutb, and Ruhollah Khomeini.

Maududi's significance lies in that he is *the* theorist of Islamic fundamentalism. His most influential work in this respect is titled *The Political Theory of Islam* [Maududi, 1976/2000], in which he specifies the characteristics of Islamic governance: "God alone is the real sovereign ... God is the real law-giver and the authority" [as cited in Moaddel & Talattof, 2000, p. 271]. Consequently, "The believers cannot resort to totally independent legislation nor can they modify any law that God has laid down" [p. 271]. Therefore, "An Islamic state must in all respects, be founded upon the law laid down by God. ... The government that runs such a state will be entitled to obedience in its capacity as a political agency set up to enforce the laws of God and only insofar as it acts in that capacity" [p. 271]. For this reason, Islamic governance [*al-dawla al-Islāmīyah*] is "theo-democratic" governance, to quote Maududi, by this he means that democracy is restricted by *Allāh*'s authority. From this angle, he sees Islamic theocracy in contrast to Christian theocracy, which was comprised of a class of priests who self-legislated laws for humans according to their whims and fancies, and who imposed their divinity upon the people under the pretext of Divine Law. As for Islamic theocracy, those who go about executing Divine Law, on Earth, are nothing but deputies for the Real Ruler. Because of this, the term "Caliphate" [*khilafah*, that is, rule under a Caliph (*khalīfah*), who is a successor to the Prophet] is used in Islam to mean that everyone who rules on Earth, under the constitution of Islam, is a deputy of the Supreme Ruler [i.e., *Allāh*]. Maududi makes the matter clearer when he says that Western secular democracy claims to be based on the will of the people; however, all of the people are participants in neither legislation nor governance. Besides, democracy separated the Islamic tradition [*al-dīn*] from politics as a result of "secularization," so it is no longer linked to morality.[23] Additionally, the concept of secularization is uncanny to Islam. Maududi's mistake here is his assumption that secularization means separating tradition from governance [*al-dawla*]. Secularization, in its essence, is thinking of human matters in relative terms and not in absolute terms—that is, *thinking of what is relative in relative terms and not in absolute terms* or not absolutizing what is relative. Religious fundamentalism, whatever form it takes, is nothing but the absolutization of the relative. Maududi's mistake also originates from his presupposition that secularization is a concept exclusive to Western civilization. This implies a binary division of civilization into a Western civilization and an Islamic civilization when civilization is a tiered singularity, the course of which goes from mythical thinking to rational thinking. Secularization is the passage to rationalism.

Sayyid Qutb went in the direction of Maududi after parting ways with Hassan al-Banna. Society, for him, is either ignorance [*jahiliyyahh*] or Islamic:

> *Jahiliyyahh* [ignorance] is the worship of some people by others ... regardless of whether these laws are against Allah's injunctions. ... Islam, on the other hand, is people's worshipping Allah alone, and deriving concepts and beliefs, laws and regulations and values from the authority of Allah Almighty, and freeing themselves from servitude to Allah's servants. [Qutb, 1964/2006, p. 146, emphasis in original]

Sayyid Qutb views, through his concept of ignorant [*jahili*] societies, that

> all the societies existing in the world today are *Jahili* ... idolatrous societies ... found in India, Japan, the Philippines. ... All Jewish and Christian societies today are also *Jahili* societies. They have

distorted the original beliefs and ascribe certain attributes of Allah to other beings. . . . Lastly, all the existing so-called "Muslim" societies are also *Jahili* societies . . . some openly declare their "secularization" and negate all their relationships with the religion; some others pay respect to the religion only with their mouths, but in their social life they have completely abandoned it. [1964/2006, pp. 91-95, emphasis in original][24]

Sayyid Qutb concludes from all of this that Islam is a

universal declaration of the freedom of man [*sic*] on the earth from every authority except that of Allah, and the declaration that sovereignty is Allah's alone and that He is the Lord of the universe, is not merely a theoretical, philosophical and passive proclamation. It is a positive, practical and dynamic message. . . . Anyone who understands this particular character of this religion will also understand the place of *Jihad bis-Saif* (striving through fighting with the sword). [1964/2006, pp. 68-71, emphasis added][25]

As such, the fundamentalist Absolute is in a bloody conflict with secularization on the pretense that secularization is the negation of *Allāh*'s sovereignty in all areas of life.

Finally, in 1979, comes Iran's Khomeini embodying this bloody fundamentalist Absolute through the establishment of the Islamic Republic of Iran. Khomeini's Najaf lectures, which he gave in 1970 between January 21 and February 8, were assembled and published in the form of a book in Farsi titled *Islamic Government*. The book centers on three issues:

1. The necessity of linking political power with Islamic objectives;

2. The duty of jurists [*fuqahā*] in establishing Islamic governance [*al-dawla al-Islāmīyah*] or the governance [*wilayah*] of the jurist;

3. A practical program for establishing Islamic governance.

These three issues revolve around a pivotal idea, which is that "divine command, has absolute authority over all individuals and the Islamic government" [Khomeini, 1970, p. 53] and that "the true rulers are the *fuqahā* themselves" [p. 56, emphasis in original]. It is the duty of the just jurist [*faqīh*] "to use government institutions to execute Divine Law [*sharī'ah*], to establish the just Islamic system" [p. 60].

Khomeini then asks about the qualities of the Muslim ruler responsible for the Islamic government, he sees two qualities ["of knowledge and justice" (1970, p. 58)]:

The first quality is that he rules based on Divine Law [*sharī'ah*] and not human will.

The second quality is that this ruler is the just jurist [*faqīh*].

From these two qualities, it can be said that the fundamentalist Absolute, for Khomeini, is embodied in the figure of the just jurist [*faqīh*]. Hence, the relative corresponds to the relative Absolute through the transference of the relative [i.e., just jurist] to the Absolute [i.e., Divine Law], or, more precisely, by the Absolutization of the relative. Any relative that remains after this Absolutization must be removed because it would constitute, then, a protrusion in the process of Absolutization. This removal is not possible without a fierce war.

Ali Shariati theorized the necessity of this war in his book *On the Sociology of Islam*, wherein he proposes: "The story of Cain and Abel is therefore the source for our philosophy of man [sic] . . . the war between two fronts that have existed throughout history" [1979, p. 98]. Hence, "The weapon of Cain has been religion, and the weapon of Abel has also been religion. It is for this reason that the war of religion against religion has also been a constant of human history" [p. 108]. If we wish to be precise, we can say it "is also the struggle between *tauhid* [monotheism] and *shirk* [polytheism]" [pp. 108–9, emphasis in original]. If the foundations of Islam are prudence [*taqiyyah*], submission to the Muslim leader [*'imām*], and martyrdom [*istishhad*], then martyrdom, in Shariati's opinion, is the most important one because it is the principle that drives the Muslim to war without hesitation. From this angle, death does not choose the martyr [*šahīd*]; it is the martyr who consciously chooses death. This is not a tragic matter but a model to follow because testimony [*šuhadā'*] by blood is the highest degree of perfection. This means that the martyr is the real Muslim.[26]

This is Islamic fundamentalism, what of Jewish fundamentalism?

Jewish fundamentalism is represented in the Gush Emunim movement. This movement was established after the 1967 war and thrived after the 1973 war. It refused the Camp David Accords because it saw Israel as a "Holy" State; hence, relinquishing any part of the land is "heresy" because each part is a grant from God [YHWH]. This holiness is not only attributed to divine wisdom but also to the Jewish blood that was spilled in wars fought in defense of Israel. For this reason, this movement called for erecting settlements in the West Bank for the purpose of returning to the origins of the Zionist Spirit.

Accordingly, their slogan was: "The greatness of Jews and their unity stem from the Greater Land of Israel." That is, the Land of Israel is the only mainstay of Judaism, and Judaism is the only mainstay of the Land of Israel.

The effects of this movement are clear in its contempt for law and order, and its refusal to obey authority unless this authority adopts strict moral standards internally and escalates confrontation externally. This is because this movement views that the world is "polluted." Consequently, it wants to renounce the culture of this age, but it is a renunciation inundated with "violence"—this platitude is the Gush Emunim movement's basic component for taking control.[27]

These are three fundamentalisms, but they are not the only fundamentalisms since there are other fundamentalisms in religions beyond these three religions. Since 1987, and for a period of eight years, the American Academy of Arts and Sciences, with funding from the John D. and Catherine T. MacArthur Foundation, embarked on a study of these fundamentalisms under the title *The Fundamentalism Project*. Five series were released from this project, which dealt with Islamic fundamentalist groups in the Middle East, North Africa, and South Asia. They also dealt with Christian fundamentalism in the Middle East, Europe, and Latin America; Jewish fundamentalism in the Middle East; Buddhist fundamentalism in Sri Lanka, Burma, and Thailand; and Hindu and Sikh fundamentalisms in the Indian subcontinent. They dealt with all of these fundamentalisms in light of their global vision, their particular understanding of science, their issued rulings on technological applications, and their opinion on the family, the law, and the constitution, as well as the extent of the influence of fundamentalism on the economy. The five series pointed to fundamentalism's refusal of the binary division between private life and public life since both must be subject to control—not mentioning the fundamentalist necessity of implementing *sharīʿah*, that is, Divine Law.

The conclusion of this series is that the emergence of fundamentalisms is not just a reaction against the new global vision, which threatens its "holy" heritage, rather it aims toward forming the world according to three sayings (violence, terrorism, and revolution) and through having control over education, the media, and establishing fundamentalist schools and institutes.

Based on all of this, it can be said that fundamentalism—whatever its religious sign may be: Christian, Islamic, Jewish, or any other ideological community—blends the Absolute with the relative and the eternal Truth with the transient truth; as such, it defends a theological truth of the past as if it were an eternal message directed against the current theological truth. So it is unable to deal with the current situation, not because it is beyond it but because it speaks about a past situation, which gives eternal credibility to a relative vision. In this context, fundamentalism becomes threatened by what I call *the clash of the Absolutes*. I say fundamentalism without mentioning the Islamic sign because this is fundamentalism whatever its religious sign may be.

The clash of the Absolutes cannot be reconciled with the call for world peace. World peace is only possible through stripping religion of dogma, that is, through the negation of dogmatism. And this negation is only possible through negating the creed sciences [*ʿulūm al-ʿaqāʾid*] because the concept of war is inherent to these sciences. Accordingly, if interfaith dialogue is based on the principles of these sciences, then it is doomed to generate religious fundamentalism. Dialogue presupposes tolerance, that is, it presumes the legitimacy of a different opinion. If differences of opinion reach the level of the Absolute, dialogue then turns into its opposite, that is, into a clash because the Absolute, by its very nature, does not accept multiplicity. The paradox here is that the multiplicity of Absolutes is threatening to these Absolutes. As a result of this threat, one Absolute must eliminate the other Absolutes. This is the logic of interfaith dialogue, which is more powerful than its good intentions.

The question remains:

What is the social class, which supports fundamentalism? I have been occupied with researching the relationship between religion and economics since December of 1974 when I published the introduction to the "Philosophy and Science" supplement to the Cairene journal *Al-Talia'a* [the Vanguard] with the title "The Tatars and Imported Thought," wherein it was reported that there is a phenomenon floating on the surface of our Egyptian society in particular and our Arab society in general, which is in need of analysis and interpretation. It is a two-dimensional phenomenon with both an economic dimension and an ideological dimension. The economic dimension is exemplified in the emergence of what I call *parasitic capitalism*. Of its signs are clandestine merchants in the consumer market and brokers who drown the nation with legally or illegally—if we wish to be more precise we can settle for illegally—imported luxury goods. Illegality centers on banning what is called *imported thought* based on the pretext of maintaining values, traditions, and what we have inherited from our elders.

The outcome of both dimensions is necessarily Tatarian. By Tatarian, I mean the old saying about the Tatars—under the leadership of Genghis Khan—being committed to one thing: the destruction of human civilization.

In 1977, I delivered a research paper in a symposium held at the Center for Middle Eastern Studies at Ain Shams University about the Arab-Israeli conflict titled "An Israeli Vision for the Future of the Region after the October War," according to which there are three currents that emerged in the Arab homeland and they are as follows:

> The first current can be labeled *the Tatarian current*. It denies civilization, doubts the power of reason, despises science, and brings to mind the Inquisition. The intent of this current is consolidating the civilizational backwardness of the Arab World.
>
> The second current can be called *the nonrevolutionary current*. It writes off the July 23, 1952 revolution for its alleged destruction of the Arab psyche, and it calls for a return to what was before the July revolution. The aim of this current is absurd since it is an attempt to change social reality.
>
> As for the third and last current, it can be named *the nonsecular current*. Its goal is toppling the Palestinian Liberation Organization's claim concerning the establishment of a secular state.

In 1975, a symposium was held with the title "Religion and Economics" and in it I put forward a development of my previous ideas in a research paper titled "Why Religion and Economics?" I posed the question as to the nature of the social class that enters into an organic relationship with religious fundamentalism. This is a necessary question based on the sine qua non between economics and religion as indicated by Max Weber in his book *The Protestant Ethic and the Spirit of Capitalism*, wherein he relates that the freedom from traditional economics contributes to a strengthening of the doubt in religious heritage and in traditional authorities, that the spirit of capitalism predates the capitalist system, and that this spirit gave birth to Protestantism. Protestantism means that one's lifestyle and what is God-given are based on the realization of obligations imposed upon humans by virtue of their place in this world, and not based on the transcendence of worldly ethics through monastic asceticism; hence, the significance of Protestantism's justification for worldly activities. In addition to this, scientific progress contributed to supporting the petite bourgeoisie in the eighteenth century. Newton's mechanics extended to all fields of human knowledge inlaid with modern mathematics, which was formulated by Leibniz and which contributed to solving the problems resulting from electricity and heat. A scientific, universal vision was established as an alternative to the religious, universal vision that dominated medieval thought.

Building on this organic relationship between Protestantism and the science-based capitalist class, we ask about the type of class that goes hand in hand with religious fundamentalism. The answer to this question is not possible without knowing the relationship between religious fundamentalism and science. Our index to knowledge of this relationship is Sayyid Qutb's saying, in his book *Islam: The Religion of the Future*, that the Ages of Rebirth (Renaissance), Enlightenment, and the Industrial Revolution disposed of not only the perceptions of the Church but also *Allāh*'s entire methodology [*manhaj*]; what Sayyid Qutb calls "hideous schizophrenia" occurred as a consequence of the separation between doctrinal perception and the system of social life. Schizophrenia is a mental illness, the most important symptoms of which are a psychic wandering in the world of fantasy and illusion, an inconsistency between one's mood and thought, and delusions. The implication of this is that European culture is an ill culture as a result of the science-based Renaissance and Industrial Revolution. Therefore, if we wanted a healthy culture, we must exclude the Renaissance, the Industrial Revolution, and science. But this exclusion demands rerouting the Renaissance-based, industry-based, and science-based capitalism to another route, which takes it out of the world of science and industry. Enlightened capitalism has morphed into a *parasitic capitalism*, which devours what is against science and reason, that is, everything that leads to absentmindedness. Nothing renders the mind absent more than drugs of all sorts and the accompanying inducers of lust and desire, which necessitate dealings in the black market. This situation led to the emergence of a new phenomenon, which can be labeled the *ordinary millionaire*, that is, it is possible for the average Joe to practice the operation of capital accumulation without production. Drug dealing comes to the forefront of this operation.

Whereas both parasitic capitalism and religious fundamentalism are destructive to the civilization of the times, whereas both are in contradiction, we are entitled to say that there is a dialectical relationship between them, that is, a relationship about which it can be said that it is both an expression of a unity and a clash of opposites.

2

What Is Secularization?

Based on what was reported in the previous chapter, it can be said that fundamentalism is opposed to secularization. Since we have elaborated on fundamentalism, we must also elaborate on secularization—hence the question: What is secularization?

In both the Arabic language and the Frankish languages, the etymology of secular is the same. In the Arabic language, the term *al-'lmānyā* is derived from *'lm* [science] as in *al-'ālm* [the world]. In the Frankish languages, it is derived from the Latin expression *saeculum*, that is, world. *Mundus* is another Latin term, which means world. The difference between both Latin terms is that *saeculum* signifies time, while *mundus* signifies space. In Latin, secular also means *cosmos* as in the universe, beauty, and order.

The term *mundus* signifies that change happens in the world and not to the world, whereas the term *saeculum* means that the world is bounded by time, that is, it has a history. Therefore, the world is bounded by time and history; the term *saeculum* is a translation of the Greek word *aiōn*, which means age or time period.

This duality in the Latin language has resulted in a theological problem, which is the sharp disagreement between the Greeks' spatial vision of existence and the Hebrews' temporal vision. The world, for the Greeks, exists in space, and events take place inside the world, but nothing happens to *the world*. Hence, they have no history of *the world*. As for the Hebrews, the world, in its essence, is history, that is, the world is *temporal*.

This contradiction between the Greeks and the Hebrews, regarding the concept of the world, was compounded during the Middle Ages by introducing the spatial or religious world over the historical or secular world. The term "secular" became confined to a narrow meaning, such as the *religious* priest who is responsible for evangelical administration being called secular. It is said, in this situation, that the priest has secularized [*t'lmn*]. The usage of the term has expanded when the emperor became independent from the bishop of Rome; and the separation, between what is spiritual and what is secular, became embodied in institutions. Some of the responsibilities of Ecclesiastical authority were transferred to political power. This transfer of power is labeled *secularization*.

However, this transference was, in its essence, an expression of a conceptual shift that took place in 1543, the year of publication of Nicolaus Copernicus's book *On the Revolutions of the Heavenly Spheres*. This history can be considered a dividing line between the end of the Middle Ages and the beginning of the modern period, since it is deeper than the event of the Turks' takeover of Constantinople or Christopher Columbus's stumbling upon the Americas. It points to the end of one world and the birth of a new world. Thanks to Copernicus, the human is no longer the center of the universe, and the universe stopped revolving around humans. Copernicus expressed this when he argued that smaller astronomical objects revolving around a motionless and larger astronomical object is a better explanation than the revolution of all astronomical objects around the Earth because if we assume that the Earth moves, which is the place from which we view celestial movement, then we get a simpler picture of the world than the one based on the assumption that celestial bodies move. As such, the human was no longer the center of the universe, and the universe was no longer supposed to be revolving around humans. That is how Copernicus uprooted the Earth and catapulted it to heaven.[1]

The decentering of the Earth was not an easy matter; take Pythagoras, for instance. He believed that the center of the world must be self-luminous because light is better than darkness, and that it must be serene because serenity is better than movement. Therefore, the Earth is not the center of the world since it is dark and has many deficiencies. Pythagoras warned his students against publicizing this theory, and he was justified in his warning because the meeting place for Pythagoreans was set on fire. It is said that Pythagoras was not present there on the day of the fire. It seems that Copernicus was aware of the dangerous consequences of adopting Pythagoras's heliocentric hypothesis, which the latter tried to hide from the public. There is no greater proof of this than Copernicus ending Book I with a letter from Lysis to Hipparchus, wherein Lysis writes:

> after Pythagoras' death his followers' brotherhood . . . have unexpectedly been scattered hither and yon . . . it is still an act of piety to recall his godlike teachings and refrain from communicating the treasures of Philosophy to those who have not even dreamed about the purification of the soul. . . . Many people even say that you [Hipparchus] are teaching philosophy publicly. This practice

was forbidden by Pythagoras, who willed his notes to his daughter Damo with an order not to turn them over to anybody outside the family. . . . They also say that when Damo died, she left the same obligation to her own daughter Bitale. Yet we of the male sex disobey our teacher and violate our oath. [as cited in Copernicus, 1543/1992, pp. 54–6][2]

I believe this conclusion indicates the reason behind his dedication of his book to Pope Paul III:

some people hear that in this volume, which I have written about the revolutions of the spheres of the universe, I ascribe certain motions to the terrestrial globe, they will shout that I must be immediately repudiated together with this belief. For I am not so enamored of my own opinions that I disregard what others may think of them. I am aware that a philosopher's ideas are not subject to the judgment of ordinary persons, because it is his endeavor to seek the truth in all things. . . . Yet I hold that completely erroneous views should be shunned. Those who know that the consensus of many centuries has sanctioned the conception that the earth remains at rest in the middle of the heaven as its center would, I reflected, regard it as an insane pronouncement if I made the opposite assertion that the earth moves. Therefore I debated with myself for a long time whether to publish the volume, which I wrote to prove the earth's motion or rather to follow the example of the Pythagoreans and certain others, who used to transmit philosophy's secrets only to kinsmen and friends, not in writing but by word of mouth. [Copernicus, 1543/1992, p. 10]

It is worth noting that he kept his heliocentric hypothesis a secret for thirty-six years.[3] Indeed, Copernicus published his hypothesis and received a printed copy of his manuscript on his deathbed on May 24, 1543. On March 5, 1616, the Congregation of the Index (the Inquisition) decreed banning Copernicus's book.

In 1609, Galileo manufactured a telescope, through which he saw the mountains on the Moon and Jupiter's four moons, and eyed their movement. In March of 1610, he published a book titled *A Sidereal Message*, wherein he declared his support for Copernicus's hypothesis. In 1613, he published a book titled *Letters on Sunspots*, which the religious authority made sure to read. They concluded that the book contains new opinions, which are in contradiction with the traditional interpretation of biblical texts. Then began the conflict between Galileo and the religious authority, so he went on to search for proofs in the Bible. However, the Holy Office declared that Copernicus is a heretic. Pope Paul V issued an order to Galileo to abstain from teaching, or defending, Copernicus's hypothesis. The latter promised to abstain; yet in 1632 he published his famous book *Dialogue Concerning the Two Chief World Systems*, in which he supported Copernicus's hypothesis and refuted Ptolemy's hypothesis, so he was summoned to Rome to face the Supreme Sacred Congregation of the Roman and Universal Inquisition, which asked him to denounce and take an oath, so he denounced and took an oath, which he signed. It is said that after signing, he put his foot to the floor and said, "And yet it moves."

In my estimation, the conflict in Europe, during the sixteenth and seventeenth centuries when Copernicus and then Galileo were alive, was between Christian fundamentalism, which adhered to the literality of the religious text and refused working reason, and secularization, which involved textual interpretation in light of working reason. Since religious fundamentalism is one of the forms of dogmatism, which fancies bearing the Absolute Truth, it can be said that the conflict during the days of Copernicus and Galileo was between dogmatism and secularization. In his foreword to Galileo's book, Einstein wrote, "The *leitmotif* which I recognize in Galileo's work is the passionate fight against any kind of dogma based on authority. Only experience and careful reflection are accepted by him as criteria of truth" [as cited in Galileo, 1632/1967, p. xvii, emphasis in original].[4] The meaning of this statement is that there is an organic relationship between de-dogmatization and secularization.

Whatever the case may be science has become, after Copernicus and Galileo, capable of forming a scientific, universal vision superseding any other vision. This implies that if science contradicts with religion then the latter must make way for the former.

Yet the issue did not stop here. The Reformation began reevaluating religious texts or, more precisely, interpreting religious texts. Its pioneer is Martin Luther whose essential idea is that the three walls of the Romanists must be destroyed if religious reform is to emerge.

The first wall is that the religious authority controls secular authority. The destruction of this wall means equalizing religious and secular authorities, and, consequently, secular authority becomes central to the formation of the Body of Christ.

The second wall revolves around religious authority being the only authority, which has the right to understand the religious text. The destruction of this wall signifies that any human being has the right to understand.

The third wall centers on the immaculacy of the Pope. Luther [1520] writes:

> Romanists want to be the only masters of Holy Scripture, although they never learn a thing from the Bible all their life long. They assume the sole authority for themselves, and, quite unashamed, they play about with words before our very eyes, trying to persuade us that the pope cannot err in matters of faith.... And if what they claim were true, why have Holy Scripture at all? Of what use is scripture?.... Therefore, the claim that only the pope may interpret Scripture is an outrageous fancied fable. [as cited in Becker, 1982, pp. 157–8]

The destruction of this wall means, for Luther, that if the Pope is actually against the Bible's teachings then it is our duty to stand for these teachings and not for the Pope; moreover, it is our duty to hold him in contempt and expel him since there is no authority in the Church except the authority of good works.[5]

After destroying the three walls, the Pope's right to interpret the Bible is denied and this interpretation becomes everyone's right. Of concern in interpretation is the negation of dogmatism, which is how secular thinking becomes legitimate.

In Russia, secularization emerged at the end of the fifteenth century during the rule of Ivan III and matured during the rule of Peter the Great when he lost confidence in the Christian clergy. After the death of Patriarch Adrian, Peter the Great opposed holding an election to choose a new Patriarch. Instead, the Most Holy Synod was created, which was subject to his sovereignty. A new ideology took the place of the Ecclesiastical ideology, which despised old-fashioned habits and ideas, derided heritage, and defended creativity and bold reforms. Peter the Great criticized the social system and had reverence for what is natural.

The effect of the emergence of secular culture was a crisis in Ecclesiastical consciousness. In overcoming the crisis, a new path for Ecclesiastical activity was unveiled, which was labeled *secularization* in the context of Ecclesiastical consciousness. As a requisite, the Church was estranged from the State, and the domain of the Church was confined to the internal life of the individual.

In light of this new consciousness, Gregory Skovoroda founded a secular Christian philosophy. He was a member of the Church, but he was a free thinker. He refused literal explanations of the Bible, and he leaned toward figurative interpretation and argued for the unity of existence. Based on his conclusion on the unity of existence, he ended up negating binary oppositions (good and evil, life and death). These dualisms are valid in the field of experience, but they do not constitute any metaphysical significance, meaning that these empirical oppositions vanish in the mystical field.

Moreover, secular culture outside of the Church was becoming stronger and more powerful. One of its pioneers was Shcherbatov Tatishchev. The starting point, for him, was the secularization of life—that is, freeing it from Ecclesiastical authority—and God's opposition to the Church since the Church prohibits humans from what Divine Law permits. For this reason, Tatishchev saw that the Church must be compliant to the State. Only then can the independence of *secular* life be realized based on *natural law*.[6]

In the eighteenth century, the Enlightenment crowned secularization. Kant's philosophy is considered to be the true expression of the spirit of the Enlightenment. He published an article in 1784 titled, *Answering the Question: "What is Enlightenment?"* Given its historical significance, here is a translated excerpt:

> *Enlightenment is [hu]man's emergence from his [or her] self-incurred immaturity. Immaturity* is the inability to use one's understanding without guidance from another. This immaturity is *self-incurred* if its cause is not lack of understanding, but lack of resolution and courage to use it without the guidance of another. The motto of enlightenment is therefore: *Sapere aude!* [Dare to understand!] Have courage to use your *own* understanding!
>
> Laziness and cowardice are the reasons why such a large proportion of men [and women], even when nature has long emancipated them from alien guidance (*naturaliter maiorennes* [Those who have come of age by virtue of nature]), nevertheless gladly remain immature for life. For the same reasons, it is all too easy for others to set themselves up as their guardians. It is so convenient to be immature! If I have a book to have understanding in place of me, a spiritual adviser to have a conscience for me, a doctor to judge my diet for me, and so on, I need not make any efforts at all. I need not think, so long as I can pay; others will soon enough take the tiresome job over for me. The guardians who have kindly taken upon themselves the work of supervision will soon see to it that by far the largest part of [hu]mankind (including the entire fair sex) should consider the step forward to maturity not only as difficult but also as highly dangerous. Having first infatuated their domestic animals, and carefully prevented the docile creatures from daring to take a single step without the leading-strings to which they are tied, they next show the danger

which threatens them if they try to walk unaided. Now this danger is not in fact so very great, for they would certainly learn to walk eventually after a few. But an example of this kind is intimidating, and usually frightens them off from further attempts.

Thus it is difficult for each separate individual to work his [or her] way out of the immaturity which has become almost second nature to him [or her]. He [or she] has even grown fond of it and is really incapable for the time being of using his [or her] own understanding, because he [or she] was never allowed to make the attempt. Dogmas and formulas, those mechanical instruments for rational use (or rather misuse) of his [or her] natural endowments, are the ball and chain of his [or her] permanent immaturity. And if anyone did throw them off, he [or she] would still be uncertain about jumping over even the narrowest of trenches, for he [or she] would be unaccustomed to free movement of this kind. Thus only a few, by cultivating their own minds, have succeeded in freeing themselves from immaturity and in continuing boldly on their way.

There is more chance of an entire public enlightening itself. This is indeed almost inevitable, if only the public concerned is left in freedom. For there will always be a few who think for themselves, even among those appointed as guardians of the common mass. Such guardians, once they have themselves thrown off the yoke of immaturity, will disseminate the spirit of rational respect for personal value and for the duty of all men [and women] to think for themselves. The remarkable thing about this is that if the public, which was previously put under this yoke by the guardians, is suitably stirred up by some of the latter who are incapable of enlightenment, it may subsequently compel the guardians themselves to remain under the yoke. For it is very harmful to propagate prejudices, because they finally avenge themselves on the very people who first encouraged them (or whose predecessors did so). Thus a public can only achieve enlightenment slowly. A revolution may well put an end to autocratic despotism and to rapacious or power-seeking oppression, but it will never produce a true reform in ways of thinking. Instead, new prejudices, like the ones they replaced, will serve as a leash to control the great unthinking mass.

For enlightenment of this kind, all that is needed is *freedom*. And the freedom in question is the most innocuous form of all—freedom to make *public use* of one's reason in all matters. But I hear on all sides the cry: *Don't argue!* The officer says: Don't argue, get on parade! The tax-official: Don't argue, pay! The clergyman: Don't argue, believe! (Only one ruler in the world says: *Argue* as much as you like and about whatever you like, but *obey*!) All this means restrictions on freedom everywhere. But which sort of restriction prevents enlightenment, and which, instead of hindering it, can actually promote it? I reply: The *public use* of [hu]man's reason must always be free, and it alone can bring about enlightenment among men [and women]; the *private use* of reason may quite often be very narrowly restricted, however, without undue hindrance to the progress of enlightenment. But by the public use of one's own reason I mean that use which anyone may make of it *as a man [or woman] of learning* addressing the entire *reading public*. What I term the private use of reason is that which a person may make of it in a particular civil post or office with which he [or she] is entrusted [Kant, 1784/2009, pp. 6–11, emphasis in original].[7]

In the late 1950s, the impact of secularization reached Christian theology and spawned a new theological movement named secular theology; some of its pioneers include Thomas Altizer and William Hamilton, both of whom published a coauthored book in 1966 titled *Radical Theology and the Death of God*.[8] They did not mean the death of God along the lines imagined by Nietzsche, in the nineteenth century, when he declared in his book *Thus Spake Zarathustra* that God is dead. What Nietzsche meant was that the traditional conception of God, wherein He is separated from the created universe, is a temporary conception because it is just a projection of the alienation that has been aching humans; it was time for transcending this alienation. As for the new conception of God, per Altizer, it is derived from Eastern religions (e.g., Nirvana, Tao, Atman, and Brahman), which are all expressions of that which is total, universal, and anti-differential. Therefore, Altizer viewed that this lack of difference, in Eastern religious thought, is not a disadvantage; on the contrary, the disadvantage is the lack of totality and universality in Christianity. For this reason, the West was unable to understand selfsame primordial consciousness, which inheres in the conception of Nirvana.

Hamilton, however, calls for reforming thought and purging it from traditional Christian formulas. Reform is possible with human maturity since only then will they not ask anything from God that the world, or its potential, cannot achieve. A sign of maturity is confidence in the world.

What followed from the emergence of secular theology is a refusal of the separation between what is sacred and what is secular or, more precisely, adapting the sacred to the secular on grounds that God is immanent and internal to the economic sphere as He is immanent to the ecclesiastical sphere.

In the first half of the twentieth century, the French school of sociology was established and led by Émile Durkheim, who focused in his research on the confrontation between the sacred and the secular, as he opined that all known religious tenets presume dividing the world into a sacred field and a secular field. Durkheim saw that there is not an entity, a subject, or an event, which is sacred; in other words, the sacred is nothing but moral and symbolic articulations, it is nothing but the projection of the collective consciousness. This means that social processes give birth to, and maintain, the sacred. Thus, Durkheim's definition of the sacred signifies the style of thought prevalent in science and in social institutions.

However, this definition is in contrast to Max Weber's vision of the sacred as embodied in religious institutions, which necessitates an examination of the sacred's relationship with other social institutions. From this perspective, the contradiction between the sacred and the secular, wherefrom originates social change, becomes one of the tools for analyzing religions. This treatment by Max Weber resulted in a sharp controversy, which emerged between social scientists and theologians in the 1960s.

In 1965, a controversial book by Harvey Cox titled *The Secular City* was published. Consequently, a rebuttal titled *The Secular City Debate* was released in 1966. Secularization, for Cox, means the transfer of responsibility from ecclesiastical authority to political authority. Therefore, it is a historical process, in which the society is liberated from the stranglehold of religion and the metaphysical vision. In that regard, Cox distinguishes the secular human from the presecular human. The presecular lives in a world of good and evil spirits. Reality, for him or her, is charged with magical power, whether beneficial or threatening. Religion here is a cosmic vision. Sumerian, Egyptian, and Babylonian religions are nothing but one of the forms of magic that unites humanity with the cosmos. History is governed by cosmology (the science of the cosmos) and society by nature—of which humans are a part. As for the secular human, he or she originated, for Cox, with the beginning of the Jewish tradition, wherein nature was separated from God, and thus the magical vision of nature, as resembling the gods, was no more. This emancipation of nature was a precondition for the evolution of natural science and for the emergence of a scientific culture. Consequently, the import of technology is not enough for lifting cultural backwardness, as the culture must be scientific. Hence, no one governs by divine justice in a secular society. Meanwhile, sociopolitical change in a society governed directly by religious symbols is impossible because this change necessitates subtracting divinity from politics. The negation of this divinity leads to a tension between religion and the social system.

Consideration remains for secularization in the Third World. The best analyst of which is American sociologist Peter Berger. In his opinion, the modern industrial state effected religious changes in non-Western societies and contributed to the spread of secularization. As for British sociologist Bryan Wilson, he sees that the decline in traditional authority and religious beliefs is attributable to colonial domination and alienation.

However, this difference between Berger and Wilson involves an agreement with regard to the importation of secularization, in Third

World societies, as a result of both the orientation of these societies toward industrialization and the modernization that accompanies said industrialization. Three characteristics of modernization can be observed:

1. Negating sacredness, that is, excluding it from defining the social world.
2. Separating religious institutions from secular institutions.
3. Transforming religious knowledge to the secular domain.

Based on these characteristics, individuals reconsider religious beliefs so that they match the demands of modernization. Whereas tribal religions in Africa and Asia do not recognize the separation between what is sacred and what is secular, this has resulted in acute problems. The political sphere is governed by religious beliefs and sacred symbols. The movements, which are trying to change these beliefs or these symbols, are questionable before the new regimes.[9]

This is a condensed presentation of the historical trajectory of secularization, from which we conclude that the definition of secularization is "thinking of what is relative in relative terms and not in absolute terms." This means dealing with human phenomena, which are necessarily relative, from a relative perspective and not from an Absolute one.

3

Fundamentalism and Secularization in the Contemporary Middle East

At the invitation to dialogue with professors of philosophy, religion, and economics, I traveled to Harvard University in April 1976. Among the discussants was Herbert Kelman, Professor of Sociology. The dialogue between us centered on a number of issues, chief among them was the issue of the Arab-Israeli conflict. Kelman asked me about my philosophical conception for solving this conflict. My answer was: "secularization is the solution." Kelman surprisingly said: "this is the first time I hear about this solution." In December 1977, *Al-Ahram* newspaper published a summary of a lecture delivered by Herbert Kelman at the American University in Cairo titled *The Psychological Impact of the Sadat Visit on Israeli Society*. In the opening of this lecture, Kelman declared: "It is fortuitous that I found myself in Israel between November 14 and 24—in other words, the period preceding, encompassing, and following President Sadat's visit there. . . . Thus, I had the opportunity to observe Israeli reactions firsthand" [Kelman, 2005, p. 118].

In this context, a round-table discussion was held on *Fundamentalism and Secularization in the Contemporary Middle East* in Brighton, England, on the occasion of convening the eighteenth World Congress of Philosophy during the last week of August 1988. Four thinkers were invited: Abderrazak Guessoum (Algeria), Muḥammad Abdul Haq (India), Adel Daher (Jordan), and Hamid Algar (United States).

I begin with Guessoum's research, which is titled *Fundamentalism and Secularization in the Islamic World Today*. The following is his text without distortion:

Any objective analysis of these two concepts (fundamentalism and secularization), around which today revolves a sharp ideological battle, necessarily requires a broader and deeper study of the social, economic, and cultural reality, which pertains to the Arab-Islamic world. What is required in order for this analysis to realize its stated aim, in my opinion, is adopting a historical, analytical, and critical approach.

There are a number of givens, among which are fundamentalism and secularization, and these givens are a translation of the mental and ideological crisis that prevails in the Islamic world today.

We are not among the proponents of some contemporary thinkers, whose opinion centers on the crisis of the Islamic world being a crisis of thought and not merely a crisis of Islamic society. We see the Arab-Islamic world suffering from a particular disease, which is an ideological crisis.

The propagators of contemporary Islamic discourse suggest, as an alternative to ideologies, the Islamic model, which is founded upon *Allāh*. It is on this basis that Islamic movements, with some exceptions, adopt a slogan like "Islamic state," "Islamic revolution," or "no authority [*sulṭān*] except *Allāh*'s authority."

From this we conclude that fundamentalism, in terms of theory, was born to fill the ideological lack that emerged from traditional structures and from the collapse of models imported from the West.

From this we also deduce that we are in the face of a problematic that emerged from comparing two cultures or civilizations, which emanated from incompatible notions. Thus, we are bound to analyzing fundamentalism as synonymous with authenticity, radicalism, and floating religious signifiers that attempt to fix the self.

There are several notions of fundamentalism: the first notion is latent in Islamic thought and leads to fixing the identity of both the individual and the society within the Muslim community [*ummah*].

The second notion is alien to Islamic thought, since it was imported by some modern Islamic thinkers from the West with the aim of curriculizing in the Islamic world.

In light of this second notion, fundamentalism means terrorism and fanaticism, which necessarily leads to a refusal of modern and contemporary life, and thus, to establishing ghettos. Therefore, the proponents of this notion suggest secularization as the alternative. Indeed, secularization became a movement since decades ago, particularly in Maghreb countries. In this research, we unravel the characteristics of this experience, which took place after the Algerian Revolution with the caveat that this experience itself was waged by the Tunisian government under the influence of Habib Bourguiba's politics, which led to shaking the social, economic, political, and cultural foundations that are rooted in the Islamic heritage.

The Islamic thinker Mohammed Arkoun [1985, p. 3] describes Bourguiba's reforms as follows:

> The national leadership, which studied in French schools and universities (Bourguiba and his colleagues as well as Mehdi Ben Barka), revealed that the failure of colonialism was disseminating liberal ideas in the context of the Age of Enlightenment in the 18th century and not in the context of traditional Islam. This is the interpretation of the bold reforms, which Bourguiba enacted after colonialism (polygamy, divorce, *Ramaḍān*, and the legal status of persons).

As such was established Western-style secularization: the separation of tradition [*al-dīn*] and governance [*al-dawla*] as a first step toward the elimination of Islamic foundations. Secularization, in Arkoun's opinion, is the greatest vehicle, before the Islamic society, for realizing progress and modernization. From this angle, secularization draws upon liberalism in the fields of economics and moral education.

The reaction to this secularization from Islamic social groups was aggressive on account that it represents a strange, dangerous, and inimical Western ideology mixed with the ideas of atheism and materialism. This violent response led to rejecting the atheism embraced by secularization, which explains the conditions for the emergence of a new fundamentalism as a means of both treating the disease of the age (i.e., atheism) and ossifying the Muslim masses. The new fundamentalists invoke the following principles:

1. Rejecting the atheistic theory of secularization, which falls under the umbrella of science;

2. Believing in one deity (oneness of *Allāh*), which would give rise to individual and social freedom because this belief entails a complete surrender to a god [*'Ilāh*], that is, a rejection of human divinity whether he or she is a colonialist or a despotic ruler;

3. Proving that Islam is the religion of science and civilization, which controls modern media to push Muslims toward the highest levels of progress;

4. Necessarily founding science on the pillars of faith; consequently, science in the Islamic understanding is nothing but a spate of faith.

The concept of fundamentalism in Islamic thought is a summary of a discourse, which links two notions: history and time. An analysis of contemporary Islamic discourse reveals to us a similarity between classic fundamentalism, which aims to purify the Arab-Islamic society of what is incompatible with the Holy Qurʾān and the prophetic accounts [*aḥādīth*], and new fundamentalism, which seeks to apply Divine Law [*sharīʿah*] to all areas of human life with the goal of being in alignment with the Divine Order.

Knowing the history of fundamentalism requires reference to the numerous confrontations between the Salafis and the fundamentalists on the one hand and the rationalists, who were influenced by Greek thought in their organization of the relationship between the religious sciences and the rational sciences, on the other hand. Here we must mention the philosophical dispute between Al-Ghazzālī [Algazelus] and Ibn Rushd [Averroës].

These confrontations did not cease through the ages, but they diverged in their paths. In the present day, Islamic thinkers are divided into two groups:

Fundamentalists who interpret change through one approach, which is the Islamic approach, and rationalists who are in compliance with secularization and sacrifice religion in exchange for scientific and technological progress. The ongoing bickering between them reveals that each group enjoys a noticeable majority. It suffices here to mention how Mohammed Arkoun considers his approach to be the farthermost from the fundamentalists' project, for he directs a scathing critique of the new *taqwaeen* [God-fearing pious ones] and the traditional *taqwaeen*; he juxtaposes all of them to the defenders of liberalism *qua* atheistic secularization.

Arkoun views that the fundamentalist school faces a difficulty, which is that its religious discourse is inadmissible because its content is nothing but ritualistic, legalistic, moralistic, and theologistic values. Therefore, Arkoun concludes that the religious mind, in Islam, stifles scientific research. What are we to think of this conclusion?

Framing the question in this way distorts facts and demonstrates a lack of understanding, whether consciously or unconsciously, in regard to religious discourse in Islam. If that is the case then how are we to interpret the scientific period, which is a sign of the progress of scientific research, when it comes to the history of Islamic thought?

Whatever the case may be, fundamentalism—in light of an objective analysis—is far from being anachronistic. On the contrary, it is quite the opposite, since it is a fertile school in terms of standards and values. Thus, it is also the mainstay of the profound significance of Arab-Islamic history.

Secularization is a concept imported from the West to signify all that is irreligious. First of all, secularization separates Church from State without perceiving other religions and non-European societies.

The emergence of secularization, as a trend in Arab-Islamic society, is an output of the Arabs' military defeat in 1967. The following slogan then became widespread: "One's secularization is a function of one's freedom from religious fanaticism."

Without a doubt, this conception is nothing but the reverberation of the laic movement, which characterizes the progress of Western European thought. Some Muslim intellectuals were impressed with Western culture and saw in its style the best approach for treating the problems of our Arab society.

Laicism builds on, in its foundation, four principal elements of human life: economics, justice, education, and political authority. In order to reveal the true depth of these fields, secularization asks us to fulfill the following aims:

Separating tradition from society through the fostering of laic education, establishing a political system that does not draw on Divine Law [*sharī'ah*], and setting up a profit-based economy.

Eliminating a genuine sector of human thought, which includes *al-nafs* [psyche, self, or soul], *al-waḥy* [revelation], and the divine secret—and with them, by necessity, the Islamic tradition [*dīn*] and ethics [*akhlaq*], which means excluding the previously mentioned sector as a whole from human thought.

For this reason, secularization faces a violent resistance from the Islamic world. All she has got then is either changing her approach or surrendering part of her defenses.

Islam, in terms of being a tolerant religion par excellence, is biased toward peaceful coexistence with other religions. As for laicism, even though it is legitimate relative to some fundamentalist Islamic movements, it is not justifiable unless it respects the principle of the freedom of creed [*'aqīdah*] and opinion.

There are movements, which express Islamic principles and work in the context of Islamic-based programs. We are witnessing, today, extensive activity from institutions that are conducting their business based on Islamic principles. The creators of these programs, or, more precisely, the founders of the fundamentalist school, struggled to effect a real change in the Islamic world.

Despite the variety of fundamentalist schools, they agree on a central idea, which is *a power grab based on an Islamic program.*

In every Islamic town, there are followers of a fundamentalist school, who are advocating for a return to the Islam from early times. Among these advocates, it is necessary to mention Jamāl al-Dīn al-Afghānī, Muḥammad 'Abduh, Rashid Rida, Muḥammad Iqbal, and Abdelhamid Ben Badis. They are all seeking to achieve two objectives:

1. Rebuilding the virtuous Islamic society liberated from all forms of slavery and inertia with the aim of realizing a much-desired unity.

2. Waking up from ideological defeat and confronting the enemies of Islam (e.g., Voltaire, Renan, and Marlow), who are carrying out hostile campaigns against Islam out of ignorance

and fanaticism, and in an effort to smear the image of the Muslim human and vilify him or her.

In addition to these advocates, there are the reformers who theorize revolutionary programs, which comprise an ideological school based on fundamentalism, and they are called: "the new fundamentalists." Among the movements supporting this ideology are the Muslim Brotherhood in Egypt, Jamaat-e-Islami in India, Dawah in Morrocco, and Wahhabism in Saudi Arabia. The leaders of these movements include Hassan al-Banna, Sayyid Qutb, Abul A'la Maududi, Ali Shariati, Malek Bennabi, and Hassan Al-Turabi.

We can get to know the program of contemporary Islamic discourse by reading the writings of the theorists of this new fundamentalism. Although this program does not infringe upon the principles of Islam or its creed, it undermines the institutions that need to be reformed. We present here the outline of Maududi's ideology:

- In individual, familial, and social life, everyone is equal before the law regardless of sex, race, or class. The law organizes all fields of life.
- Islamic economics is the third way between capitalism and communism, and it invokes three principles:
  1. Inheritance
  2. Alms-giving [*al-zakat*]
  3. Canceling usury
- The principles of Islamic governance:
  - *Sharī'ah* is the Supreme Law dominating all fields.

– Political authority is in the hands of the pious ones [*saleheen*].

This is the outline of the fundamentalist perspective in the Islamic world today. As for the concept of secularization, it is a movement that has its advocates; nevertheless, it started to lose steam—not mentioning losing its place in the Arab-Islamic world to the new fundamentalists. However, this battle between fundamentalism and secularization is onerous and will not be resolved soon.

Next is Muḥammad Abdul Haq's research, which is titled *The Roots of Islamic Fundamentalism in Egypt*. In his opinion, the story of modern Islamic thought in Egypt is the story of the confrontation between traditional Islam and Western civilization during the nineteenth and twentieth centuries. This confrontation has led to social, economic, and cultural changes; these changes in turn resulted in a conflict among the minds of intellectuals. The Christian intelligentsia adopted secularization, such as Shiblī Shumayyil, Farah Antun, and Salama Moussa—the strongest defender of social Darwinism in Egypt. As for the nationalists, like Mustafa Kamil and Saad Zaghloul, they were influenced by Jamāl al-Dīn al-Afghānī and struggled for national independence. On the religious level, the Western influence led to the division of "scholars" [*'ulamā'*] into two groups: one in favor of change in response to the Western challenge and the other, represented by Al-Azhar University, in opposition to everything that is Western. This conflict is not the first of its kind endured by Islam. It happened before during the Middle Ages as a consequence of the Hellenic influence and has resulted in the formation of apologetic theology [i.e., Islamic scholasticism or *'ilm al-kalām*], which is a science that tried to accommodate that which could not be accommodated, so the fundamentalists ruled it out. The conflict facing Islam, in this age, culminated in the emergence of nationalist, secular, and religious tendencies. Muḥammad Abdul Haq partitions and separates the religious tendency while remarking that the old conflict was philosophical and produced rationalism. As for the current conflict, it is political and produced nationalism in the face of colonialism. The nationalists lived in harmony with the traditional scholars. As for the modernists, the colonial authorities supported them. As such, the Islamic intelligentsia lives, today, in a state of schizophrenia as a result of the modernists' attempt to integrate Western liberal and secular ideas with Islam's philosophical structure, therefore, creating a new synthesis. Among these modernists are Hasan al-Attar, Abd al-Rahman al-Jabarti, and Rifaʻa al-Tahtawi. They internalized Western civilization during the French occupation of Egypt; they tried reconciling science with tradition and reframed Islamic scholasticism [*ʻilm al-kalām*] as liberating Islamic society from the shackles of heritage [*al-turath*]. Muḥammad ʻAbdu and his modernist followers, who founded what is known as the "Muḥammad ʻAbdu school of Islamic Modernism," followed suit. Nonetheless, a liberal trend—more radical in its interpretation of Islamic values—opposing the teachings of Muḥammad ʻAbdu was established; spearheading this trend were Sheikh Ali Abdel Raziq, Khalid Mohamed Khalid, and Taha Hussein (at the beginning of his life). Their books provoked the wrath of Al-Azhar, who accused them of aberration and atheism.

The central idea, for the proponents of this radical trend, is distinguishing between the spiritual and the temporal or, more precisely, between Islamic rites and praxis. This distinction paved the way for establishing the secular foundations of Islam, which denote temporal matters succumbing to a humanistic vision; therefore, it is necessary to implement legal reasoning [*al-ijtihād*] in solving them, that is, implementing human reasoning. The guiding principle in legal reasoning is human well-being.

The liberal school did not run its course since it quickly found itself in an alliance with the colonial authority that was in confrontation with the nationalists. As such, the school failed to consolidate Islamic liberalism with political freedom and faced resistance from a conservative and reactionary force, whose ideology reverts back to the teachings of the fundamentalists from the Islamic Middle Ages. In 1930, this force succeeded in forming fundamentalist organizations, such as the Muslim Brotherhood [*al-Ikhwān al-Muslimūn*], which Hassan al-Banna established in 1928, and Young Egypt [*Misr al-Fatah* or Egypt, The Young Girl], which Ahmed Hussayn established in 1933. Its goal was resisting Westernization and evangelism. One of its repercussions was the confiscation in 1925 of Sheikh Ali Abdel Raziq's book, *Islam and the Foundations of Governance*, in which the Sheikh called for secularization and critiqued the politicization of Islam. Here Muḥammad Abdul Haq refers to a quote from George Shehata Anawati stating that the weapons of nationalism obliged some Christians to defend the official religion [i.e., Islam] to demonstrate their patriotism. The secular Salama Moussa said, "My duty is to defend my country's religion" and Makram Ebeid said, "I am Christian in terms of religion and Muslim in terms of nationality." Taha Hussein wrote a three-part series about the Prophet [*al-nabī*, i.e., Muḥammad], titled *The Prophet's Life* [*'ala hamish al-sīra* or On the Sidelines of the (Prophet's) Biography]. Mohammed Hussein Heikal, the editor-in-chief of the liberal newspaper *Al Siyasa* [*Politics*], wrote a book titled *The Life of Muhammad* [*ḥayat Muḥammad*]. Abbās al-Aqqād released the Geniuses [*al-Abqarīyat*] book series beginning with *The Genius of Muhammad* [*Abqarīyat Muḥammad*]. These thinkers themselves are the ones who led the campaign against dogmatism and reactionism. In 1930, they gave up on the issue of enlightenment and surrendered to the fundamentalists. Religious fervor crystallized in the writings of Rashid Rida, the pioneer of the new Wahhabi Salafi movement and the editor-in-chief of *al-Manar* [the Lighthouse]. The central idea, in these writings, is the politicization of Islam since it is his creed that Islam ceases to be without the establishment of international Islamic governance, which would include the entire Muslim community [*ummah*] under the rule of a Caliph/Sultan. Rashid Rida, from this angle, is considered the trailblazer for the Muslim Brotherhood, rather the trailblazer for a Salafi movement, which condemns heresy and glorifies the pious predecessors [*al-salaf al-ṣāliḥ*]. What is meant by *al-salaf* is the first three generations of Muslims beginning with the Prophet Muḥammad (*ṣalawāt*), his companions [the *Sahabah*], their successors [the *Tabi'un*], and the successors of the successors [the *Taba Tabi'in*]. The pioneers of Salafism, as a matter of fact, are the first Hanbalis fronted by Ibn Taymiyyah (1263–1368) and Ibn Qayyim al-Jawziyya (1292–1350). Ibn Taymiyyah is designated the renewer [*mujaddid*] of the thirteenth century. Renewal [*tajdid*] here is the return to a pure Islam before heresy polluted it. This means that divine will is not going to be realized by following Divine Law [*al-sharī'ah*] as a means to individual salvation but by establishing a virtuous [*fadil*] society, thanks to the collective will of the Muslim community [*ummah*].

The Salafi movement was quickly influenced by Wahhabism, which appeared in the Kingdom of Saudi Arabia under the leadership of Muḥammad ibn Abd al-Wahhab and paved the way for Salafism in Egypt, India, and Indonesia. But ultimately it goes back to Ibn Taymiyyah and Ibn Qayyim al-Jawziyya, and its slogan is: "No sultan, but *al-Qur'ān* and *al-sunnah* [the way of life based on Muḥammad's words or acts]; no creed [*'aqīdah*] except the oneness of *Allāh* [*al-tawḥīd*]."

Muḥammad Abdul Haq views Salafism as fundamentalism, but, for him, it is innovative in the sense that it rejects dogmatism by way of tradition, and it calls for a new superstructure of juristic interpretations [*al-fiqh*] founded upon "the Book [*al-Kitāb*, that is, *al-Qur'ān*] and *al-sunnah* [normative precedents of the earliest Muslim community]" along with modern interpretations.

With the appearance of the Muslim Brotherhood, Islam was politicized and the following slogan was raised: "*al-Qur'ān* is our constitution, struggle [*al-jihad*] is our path, and death for *Allāh*'s sake is our highest aspiration." Hassan al-Banna was opposed to democracy and socialism and sided with Nazism. In 1940, al-Banna established a secret terrorist apparatus named "the secret apparatus" to defend Islam with funding from Germany. Al-Banna called for a restructuring of what he named "the Islamic system" as an alternative to what he designated "the ignorant [*al-jāhilī*] system." With the death of al-Banna, the hostile vision was developed further under the influence of Abul A'la Maududi via Sayyid Qutb.

Adel Daher's research, *Philosophy against Islamic Fundamentalism*, follows next. Daher views that we got used to—in our handling of anti-secularist Islamic fundamentalism—ignoring epistemological problems, while being satisfied with responding to them sociohistorically. This satisfaction is likely to make us forget the fundamentalists' chief argument, which is that *we cannot deal with worldly affairs without divine guidance.*

Some secularists draw on religious arguments, *al-Qur'ān*, and *al-sunnah* to show that *Allāh* did not intend to organize our worldly affairs on the basis of religious doctrine. These arguments are legitimate, but they are not decisive because we can probably find *Qur'ānic* verses [*āyāt*] or prophetic accounts [*'aḥādīth*], which support both the affirmative and the negative. And if we add historical evidence to the fundamentalist interpretation of the religious text, then it becomes clear to us that religious arguments are not decisive when it comes to supporting secular interpretation.

In his opinion, there is a conclusive argument in the critique of Islamic fundamentalism, which is rejecting its latent epistemological theory: that humanity is qualified to know the right path for organizing its worldly affairs with divine guidance.

Fundamentalists claim that Islam, unlike the other monotheistic traditions, is not only concerned with human salvation but also with socially, politically, economically, and culturally organizing worldly life. This is a harmless argument if we view it as a historical argument about Islam given that, since its inception, Islam was forced to link the spiritual with the non-spiritual. From this angle, one may not object. But what one may object to is the allegation that Islam adopts the idea of theocratic (divine) governance.

The fundamentalists' problem revolves around them wanting to transform what is historical to what is "logical" meaning that they have a firm belief, which is that Islam provides us with answers to all the important questions pertaining to worldly affairs regardless of historical context. Accordingly, the fundamentalists' stance toward secularization is that it is to be rejected not only from the religious angle but also from the epistemological angle. In other words, their stance centers on, one can say, that "knowing" how to organize worldly affairs is derived from "religious knowledge." If we call this knowledge "practical knowledge," this means that the basis of practical human knowledge is latent within religious knowledge. Here we raise three questions:

> First: What are the principal elements of practical knowledge?
>
> Second: What is the meaning of religious knowledge?
>
> Third: Are any of the elements of practical knowledge based in religious knowledge?

To the first question, Daher answered that practical knowledge signifies knowing ends and means. For example, if we wanted to organize a society capitalistically or socialistically then we have to identify the end behind this organization and the means for realizing this end. Knowing ends is normative, and ultimately moral, because what needs to be known is that: things are acceptable the way they are, they are socially significant, or they must be changed. If knowing ends presupposes a theoretical scientific knowledge, then knowing means presumes scientific knowledge or, more precisely, applied scientific knowledge. Therefore, one can say that theoretical scientific knowledge is contained within practical knowledge, which can be sociological if it is related to society or physical if it is related to the physical environment. Thus, practical knowledge contains a scientific—as well as normative and moral—knowledge of a sociological or physical nature.

Daher then examines the conception of religious knowledge to see what this knowledge entails. By religious knowledge, he means the knowledge pertaining to the Judeo-Christian heritage, which is part of Islam. In the context of this heritage, the final theme for religious knowledge is *Allāh*, the Eternal, the Almighty, the Good, the Free, and the Source of the moral compulsion. However, religious knowledge does not end here, rather it transcends toward a knowledge of the attributes, acts, and intentions of *Allāh* since these all flow from, and are determined by, the essence of *Allāh*.

In other words, one can say that the essence of *Allāh*, beyond which there is nothing, is what determines His attributes, acts, and intentions. Hence, if we say that these are essential then we mean that it is illogical for *Allāh* not to possess them. This is a logical proposition regarding religious issues. From this angle, this logical proposition ultimately reveals to us that practical knowledge cannot be founded upon religious knowledge. The reason for this is that the issues of practical knowledge do not share the same logical proposition as that of religious issues, since they appear to be contingent but not necessary. Therefore, they cannot be established epistemologically except with regard to propositions concerning their nature, that is, it is absurd to derive issues of practical knowledge from religious issues since these are necessary, and necessity is a logically inherited characteristic. Logical inheritance means that the type of characteristic contained in premises must be carried through to the conclusion if the reasoning is correct because correct reasoning logically invalidates for there to be true premises and a false conclusion. The question then becomes:

What is the logical proposition for issues of practical knowledge?

The possibility of falsifying practical issues, to begin with, is conceivable in the sense that being in a situation that allows us to know that practical issues are true does not mean that there are no knowable conditions, which allow us to say that these issues are false. From this we deduce two outcomes: first, what is scientific is falsifiable and, second, what is false is knowable.

Even from a theistic perspective, the possibility of falsifying what is scientific is not in doubt. If what is scientific is a matter of causality, then characterizing it as necessary limits the capacity of *Allāh*. *Allāh*'s allness—to the extent that He is, in essence, the Almighty—has to do with His will. But this saying is not enough since if effects essentially overflow from His effectual nature then the Existent, who creates a pattern from causes, will not permit for an Other, including Himself, to suspend this pattern.

As concerning normative moral issues, their sincerity depends on numerous factors: human nature, human needs, and sociohistorical circumstances. But all of these are not of a fixed essence; as such, these issues can possibly be false.

If we agree on scientific and normative issues being contingent, as opposed to necessary, then it is inconsistent to say that scientific and normative issues are derived from divine matters since these matters are necessary, and necessity is hereditary. If practical knowledge is attributable to scientific and normative knowledge, then it is contradictory to say that the basis for practical knowledge is religious knowledge.

There is another argument, which can be considered the death of fundamentalism. This argument is based on an axiom, which is that the concept of *Allāh* is a normative concept, since *Allāh*, in Islam, is necessarily the only Existent worthy of worship. It is necessary for an Existent like that to be attributed with moral perfection in addition to other attributes. However, we cannot know that *Allāh* exists unless we are capable of identifying the correct norms for distinguishing between good and evil, true and false, and identifying, in general, if a given person holds these norms by virtue of their essence, intentions, and acts. This indicates that morality precedes religion from the standpoint of tradition, if not also historically. And if that is the case, and if we have succeeded in demonstrating that practical knowledge is independent of religious knowledge, then scientific knowledge has no basis whatsoever in religious knowledge.

Concerning this epistemological dilemma, which faces the fundamentalist, there is another path that they can tread to avoid falling into this dilemma. Namely, the fundamentalist perceives that the matter at hand is not an epistemological matter but a matter of the commands that *Allāh* wants us to implement, the manner in which our relationship with *Allāh* is supposed to be, and the way we are to respond to *Allāh*'s commands.

In other words, one can say that it is not a question of the epistemological relationship between morality and tradition, rather between the human and their Creator. Daher refutes this question beginning with the following axiom: *Allāh* is the Source of the moral compulsion. Therefore, one has a duty to obey *Allāh* since He is our Creator. Therefore, it is imperative that we adhere to His commands without deviating from them. In addition to this axiom, there is another one: *Allāh*'s command for us is to organize society in the fields of politics, law, and economics on the basis of Islam. The outcome of these two axioms, then, is that *it is imperative for the Muslim to organize society based on the principles of Islam.*

This argument is not without objections, for there is a proliferation of Islamist thinkers who do not consider this argument to be backed by the precepts of Islam. Even if we ignore this proliferation, the argument that *it is imperative for the Muslim to organize society based on the principles of Islam* is not aligned with the divine creed since it removes from the mind its normative function, which is a function that Islam recognizes. Because if *Allāh*'s intention was for the human to know their Creator, and if moral knowledge is essential for knowing *Allāh*, then the function of the mind is to be normative. Of significance to this function is for the mind to be able to identify ends without *Allāh*'s assistance.

In contrast to Daher's research is Hamid Algar's research, which is titled *Remarks on Islamic Fundamentalism*. He sees that the current movement of militant religious revival, which is prevailing throughout the Islamic world, resulted in generalizations most of which are hostile. In fact, rejecting Islamic fundamentalism, on the supposition that it is the enemy of "modernity," reminds one of the nineteenth century's blatant outcry against "fanatic Muslims" who were resisting Christian Europe's momentous victory. The ideological color of the Western fervor for domination has changed, but the response to Islamic resistance has not since the West forges, distorts, and attacks, while simultaneously alleging that it is morally superior.

In order for us to understand the situation of contemporary Islam, we must mention the following points:

1. Recognizing the diversity of conditions in the Islamic world. Meaning that the current religious revival among Muslims

in China, for example, must be appreciated according to its specific framework, which is distinct from Hezbollah's resistance in Lebanon. As such, the current stage of Islamic revival is not merely a reaction against an abstract and total understanding, which is said to be "modernity"; Islamic history is a function of its own internal activity in this world.

2. If we mean by "fundamentalism" a movement similar to Christian fundamentalism as to what it involves in terms of a focus on the literal understanding of the Holy Book, then we must remember that Islamic fundamentalism is nothing but a creature existing in the mind of Western analysts since it has no existence in the external world. Islamic movements are not concerned with what is marginal in society, but they derive their appeal from the radical reformulation of social problems and ambitions.

3. Saying that Islamic movements as a whole aspire to return to models of the State, which are beyond time, is a false statement. It is true that there were periods in Islamic history, which involved normative values, but—with the exception of some cases—there is no instrumental attempt to simulate a sociopolitical system, which was prevalent from time immemorial. The desired ideal is of establishing "Islamic modernity," which is a powerful and comprehensive expression and a mainstay of the independence of Islamic peoples.

4. Saying that Islamic movements are resigned to "violence" is a distortion resulting from a Western imagination about

contemporary Islam. Armed struggle is the choice of a few Islamic movements. Violence is pointed at Muslims generally when they are not its promoters. Even the Islamic Republic of Iran was established from a movement, whose basis is the Muslim's willingness to die as a martyr and not from a desire to kill. Nevertheless, Iran's Islamic system—in the Western imagination—is mindless fanatic violence.

Nothing remains after that except my research, which is titled *The Fundamentalist Absolute and Secularization in the Contemporary Middle East*. This research, by virtue of its title, necessitates a clarification of its key terms: "the Absolute" and "secularization."

Kant is the first to introduce the concept of the Absolute in the field of philosophy, namely in the first edition of his book *Critique of Pure Reason*. He says that the mind, through knowing, is bound to face matters it cannot possibly avoid. These matters are imposed on the mind, by its very nature; however, it is incapable of responding to them. They are put forward without a response and they revolve around incontrovertibly grasping the Absolute. As such, Kant distinguishes between two conditions: the condition of searching for a grasp of the Absolute and the condition of grasping the Absolute—partly because the Absolute, once it is grasped, becomes relative and ceases to be accommodating for reality as a whole.

Nonetheless, Hegel's philosophy arrived expressing the concept of the Absolute, unlike Kant's conception, since Hegel views that nature as a whole reveals the Absolute when it is in a condition of self-alienation. Nature is a field, in which things separate from one another while deludedly thinking that they are autonomous; as a result they stay away from the Absolute, which is the unit clamping down on everything. F. H. Bradley went in the same direction: religion and philosophy, for him, are both signifiers and signifieds of the Absolute. Philosophy shows us that science is a meager thing, which is superfluous to the richness of existence. Religion attempts to conceptualize the Absolute in itself via meanings based on experience. Thus, the Absolute, for Bradley, assumes a religious nature; it is nothing but an extension of George Berkeley's religious Absolute or, more precisely, the divine mind, which offers us meanings and their exemplifications. The divine will is the one who establishes relationships among them. Nature, in the end, is nothing but the language with which God speaks to us. However, with the beginning of the twentieth century, belief in this sort of Absolute declined.

From our understanding of the meaning of the Absolute, we can delimit *the fundamentalist Absolute* as not the abstract Absolute removed from the march of history but *the Absolute immanent to history: controlling its course, freezing it in the past, hence, amputating from time its timeliness, that is, the future.* Therefore, Bradley qualifies war as holy and necessary.

After that, secularization has to be tackled. *Al-'lmānyā* in Arabic is derived from *'lm* [science] as in *al-'ālm* [the world]. In Frankish, it is derived from the Latin expression *saeculum*, that is, the world as sliced by time, which is history. From here, secularization can be defined as "thinking of what is relative in relative terms and not in absolute terms." From this perspective, one can identify its genesis in 1543. In this year, a new mentality emerged as a result of Copernicus's and Galileo's formation of a new cosmology. Copernicus's book, *On the Revolutions of the Heavenly Spheres*, was published toward the end of his life in 1543. In the book, the human was no longer the center of the cosmos, and the cosmos no longer revolved around the human.

Based on the foregoing, the fundamentalist Absolute is arguably in contradiction with secularization; therefore, fundamentalism is not conservatism since conservatism accepts reducing the salience of religion and theology and, thus, is not incompatible with modernity—fundamentalism rejects the modern mind. Its objective is not translating religion to the discourse of modernity but changing this discourse so that it becomes possible for religion to represent it. Moreover, the essence of fundamentalism is the belief that the world as a whole, and not merely the religious portion of it, must reflect its divine source. For this reason, a contemporary movement was established in the West to fight religious fundamentalism; it is known as "secular humanism," and it has ten principles:[1]

1. Free Inquiry: "truth is more likely to be discovered if the opportunity exists for the free exchange of opposing opinions. . . . This applies not only to science and to everyday life, but to politics, economics, morality, and religion."

2. Separation of Church and State: "A pluralistic, open democratic society. . . . Clerical authorities should not be permitted to legislate their own parochial views—whether moral, philosophical, political, educational, or social."

3. The Ideal of Freedom: "We stand not only for freedom from religious control but for freedom from jingoistic government control as well."

4. Ethics Based on Critical Intelligence: "ethical judgments can be formulated independently of revealed religion . . . ethical

conduct is, or should be, judged by critical reason.... We are opposed to absolutist morality."

5. Moral Education: "We do not believe that any particular sect can claim important values as their exclusive property.... We wish to encourage wherever possible the growth of moral awareness and the capacity for free choice.... We do not think it is moral ... to impose a religious creed on young people before they are able to consent."

6. Religious Skepticism: "we are generally skeptical about supernatural claims.... We are doubtful of traditional views of God and divinity.... We consider the universe to be a dynamic scene of natural forces that are most effectively understood by scientific inquiry.... We do not accept as true the literal interpretation of ... religious documents."

7. Reason: "We view with concern the current attack by nonsecularists on reason and science. We are committed to the use of the rational methods of inquiry, logic, and evidence in developing knowledge and testing claims to truth ... we are open to the modification of all principles."

8. Science and Technology: "We believe the scientific method ... is still the most reliable way of understanding the world. Hence, we look to the natural, biological, social, and behavioral sciences for knowledge of the universe and man's [sic] place within it. Modern astronomy and physics have opened up exciting new dimensions of the universe: they have enabled humankind to explore the universe by means of space travel.... We are thus opposed in principle

to any efforts to censor or limit scientific research without an overriding reason to do so. While we are aware of, and oppose, the abuses of misapplied technology and its possible harmful consequences."

9. Evolution: "Today the theory of evolution is again under heavy attack by religious fundamentalists.... This is a serious threat both to academic freedom and to the integrity of the educational process."

10. Education: "In our view, education should be the essential method of building humane, free, and democratic societies. ... Among its vital purposes should also be an attempt to develop the capacity for critical intelligence in both the individual and the community."

We conclude from all of this that there are two chief movements in the second half of the twentieth century, and they are religious fundamentalism and secular humanism—hence, the significance of the issue at hand in this symposium, that is, *Fundamentalism and Secularization in the Contemporary Middle East*. However, this title does not mean that fundamentalism and secularization are limited to the Middle East, for they are global phenomena. It means, however, taking the Middle East region as a model for examining these two phenomena.

4

Postmodernism and Fundamentalism

If fundamentalism is anti-secular, and if secularization is the hallmark of modernism, then fundamentalism is antimodern. What is intended by modernism, in Daniel Bell's opinion, is getting away from the authority of the past, diminishing the scope of the sacred, and following the Faustian spirit when it comes to general knowledge.[1]

Peter Berger goes further than Bell; he views modernism as a type of heresy, particularly in the Third World, because it unsettles traditional values that are based on fate [*al-qadr*, or divine destiny]. From time immemorial, sex and procreation were tied to fate. Modernism came on the scene, denied fate, and advocated choice. There is a difference between fate and choice. In the first case, the feature of certainty substantially characterizes social institutions. There is but one way of dealing with social matters, marriage, child rearing, and the exercise of power. As for the second case, there are alternatives, hence a multiplicity. The modern human is faced with multiple choices in the field of action, rather in the field of thinking.

The question remains:

Is postmodernism antimodern?

The expression "post" traditionally means connection without separation. This expression was added first to the term "physis" [nature] as in "metaphysis" [post-nature]. The coinage of this term can be attributed to one of the followers of Aristotle, who was concerned with organizing his writings and found fourteen books numbered according to the Greek alphabet, which comprise three major research projects: the principles of knowledge, Being's generalities, and the prime mover. These projects fell sequentially after "physics," so this follower called them "metaphysics" based on their arrangement. Herein lies the connection between "physics" and "metaphysics": understanding the book *Metaphysics* is not possible without reading *Physics*.

However, connection does not signify coherence between the anterior and the posterior; it means parting. We may imagine parting as separation. However, the truth of the matter is that what parted is a negation of that from which it parted, that is, the posterior's negation of the anterior.

Some say, for example, "post-industrial society," which is the expression of American sociologist Daniel Bell, rather it is the title of his book, *The Coming of the Post-Industrial Society*, which was originally a research paper that he presented at an international conference in Zurich in June 1970. Bell means with this expression the transformation of modern society from the production of goods to a service economy, the establishment of theoretical knowledge as the source of creativity, a new rational technology, and changing the social structure.

Moreover, some claim "post-historical," which is a term coined by Japanese scholar Francis Fukuyama that appeared in his 1989 article, *The End of History?*, wherein he establishes that there are essential events in the current world-historical period, which are the reform movements in the Soviet Union and Eastern Europe as well as the dissemination of consumer culture. These events are evidence of "The triumph of the West, of the Western *idea*" [Fukuyama, 1989, p. 3, emphasis in original]. He goes on to say:

> What we may be witnessing is not just the end of the Cold War, or the passing of a particular period of postwar history, but the end of history as such: that is, the end point of mankind's [sic] ideological evolution and the universalization of Western liberal democracy as the final form of human government. [Fukuyama, 1989, p. 4][2]

Further, others assert "post-capitalist society," which is a phrase coined by American scholar Peter Drucker, and it revolves around the emergence of new multiplicities—that is, multiplicities never before seen—that create new demands for political leadership. In the past, the organ of power was one, but now it is plural and transnational [cf. Drucker, 1993, p. 9]. This multiplicity is grounded in organizations that have one defined purpose.

The question following from this is:

What is the meaning of the term "postmodernism"?

We begin with identifying the meaning of "modernism" then we follow with delimiting the significance of "postmodernism." Modernism, in the *Oxford English Dictionary*, means new approaches; believing in science, planning, secularization, and progress; coveting symmetry and stability; and trusting in infinite progress.

From this perspective, modernism—in its genesis—can be attributed to both English philosopher Francis Bacon and French philosopher René Descartes. Bacon [1620/2004] laid down a new logic for constituting a new mind purged from what he termed idols, "the idols of the mind," of which there are four kinds:

> The *idols of the tribe* are founded in human nature itself and in the very tribe or race of mankind [*sic*]. The assertion that the human senses are the measure of things is false; to the contrary, all perceptions, both of sense and mind, are relative to man [*sic*], not to the universe. . . . The *idols of the cave* are the illusions of the individual man [*sic*]. For . . . each man [*sic*] has a kind of individual cave or cavern which fragments and distorts the light of nature. . . . [The] *idols of the marketplace*; we take the name from human exchange and community. Men [*sic*] associate through talk; and words are chosen to suit the understanding of the common people. And thus a poor and unskilful code of words incredibly obstructs the understanding. . . . [The] *idols of the theatre*, for all the philosophies that men [*sic*] have learned or devised are, in our opinion, so many plays produced and performed which have created false and fictitious worlds. [pp. 41–2, emphasis in original]

After the mind is purged from these idols, it goes on to using the inductive method, which relies on experimenting.

As for Descartes [1637/2006], he established a new approach that is based on the mind's commitment to clear and distinct ideas as well as on doubt in all human knowledge except doubt itself: "while I was trying to think of all things being false in this way, it was necessarily the case that I, who was thinking them, had to be something; and observing this truth: *I am thinking therefore I exist* [*cogito ergo sum*], was so secure and certain" [p. 219, emphasis in original]. It means that the human is a self-defined independent creature.

After Descartes, there were theorists with divergent views on this truth [i.e., *cogito ergo sum*] from John Locke to Kant. They were all aware of modernity. Nevertheless, modernity was not at the forefront of philosophical thought until the end of the eighteenth century when Hegel proposed it as a philosophical issue. From this angle, one can say that Hegel is the first philosopher to elaborate a clear conception of modernity. Therefore, we must begin with him if we want to understand the intimate relationship between modernism and rationalism. Hegel conceives the centrality of self-consciousness as the determinant for philosophizing in the modern age, and that this consciousness—in its progress—is not subject to chance but to law. He says:

> The facts within that history [of Philosophy] . . . are not a mere collection of chance events . . . in the activity of thinking mind there is real connection, and what there takes place is rational. It is with this belief in the spirit of the world that we must proceed to history, and in particular to the history of Philosophy. [Hegel, 1892, p. 19][3]

In light of this elucidation of modernism, a group of religious philosophers was established under the leadership of Alfred Loisy and Edouard Le Roy; its purpose was accepting Church doctrine— whatever interpretation was being imposed—as long as the Church was separated from the State and faith was separated from the mind. Nevertheless, this color of modernism was violently condemned by

Pope Pius X in 1907. The impact of this condemnation is that Catholic intellectuals panicked, and a trend seeking to avoid authentic thinking out of fear that it may lead to heresy became widespread. Nonetheless, two directions by two German philosophers represent an authentic riposte to modernism: one led by Nietzsche, and the other led by Heidegger.

Nietzsche critiqued the cult of reason, which revolved around the mind's delusion that it is capable of knowing the truth and existence. Since logic, which is a product of the mind, is an illusion, and the mind's principles are its invention, he alleges that these are the laws of existence. Therefore, there are no pillars that can be intellectually justified. But there are perspectives, confirmations, and rebuttals. Nature narrows down the space of a perspective, thereby decreasing the space of freedom. Moreover, "To be sure, to speak of spirit and the good . . . meant standing truth on her head and denying *perspective* itself, the basic condition of all life" [Nietzsche, 1886/1990, p. 52, emphasis in original].[4]

As for Heidegger, his direction centers on modernism having forgotten to ask about Being, which was of concern to both Plato and Aristotle. He asks in his 1927 book *Being and Time*:

> Do we in our time have an answer to the question of what we really mean by the word "being"? Not at all. So it is fitting that we should raise anew *the question of the meaning of Being*. But are we nowadays even perplexed at our inability to understand the expression "Being"? Not at all. So first of all we must reawaken an understanding for the meaning of this question. [Heidegger, 1927/1962, p. 19, emphasis in original]

Then he continues by saying that time is "the possible horizon for any understanding whatsoever of Being" [Heidegger, 1927/1962, p. 19]. Time does not imply determinism, rather it signifies contingency.

Twenty years later, Heidegger published an essay titled *Letter on Humanism*, which is addressed to a French philosopher by the name of Jean Beaufret, wherein he discusses the "oblivion of Being" or "homelessness" as well as "humanism" being the main reason for "strife."[5]

In this context, the meaning of postmodernism can be specified. However, there is a difficulty facing us, which is the ambiguity of this meaning due to the proliferation of definitions. Michael Kohler (1977) presented these definitions in his essay, "*Postmodernismus*": *Ein begriffsgeschichtlicher Überblick*, and the most important ones are Irving Howe's (1959) definition in his article "Mass Society and Post-Modern Fiction" as well as Harry Levin's (1960) definition in his essay *What Was Modernism?* For Howe [1959, p. 427], postmodernism signifies the erosion of traditional centers of authority, the neglect of traditional ceremonies, and the loss of strong beliefs. Consequently, "the connection between subject and setting cannot always be made, and the 'individual' of their novels, because he [*sic*] lacks social definition and is sometimes a creature of literary or even ideological fiat, tends to be not very individualized" [p. 433]. Therefore, these novels "illustrate the painful, though not inevitable, predicament of rebellion in a mass society" [p. 435]. As for Levin [1960], postmodernism is a synonym for "stupidity" [p. 627].

In the mid-1960s, Leslie Fiedler felt that we must consider the rupture of traditional values, mentioned by Howe, as not negative but positive because postmodernism finally amputated the relationship between modernist writers and the elite. It poses a "new sensibility," in the words of Susan Sontag, who joins Fiedler in his opposition to semantics. She argued in her 1966 book, *Against Interpretation and Other Essays*, that "[i]t doesn't matter whether artists intend, or don't intend, for their works to be interpreted" [p. 27] and that "[i]n place of a hermeneutics we need an erotics of art" [p. 38]. For Sontag, what characterizes postmodernism is an escape from interpretation. In order for art to realize this escape, what is subsequently required of it is for art to not be art so that it resists interpretation. This is the divide between modernism and postmodernism, whereby modern art points to the deep meaning latent below the surface.

As for Richard Wasson, he presented a new perspective on postmodernism in the mid-1960s with his 1969 article *Notes on a New Sensibility*, wherein he viewed postmodernism as a revolt against modernism. Iris Murdoch, Alain Robbe-Grillet, and John Barth represent this revolt. The central idea for them revolves around a skepticism toward modern sensibility and modern semantics, particularly "metaphor" creating "a truth different from that of rational and empirical methodology" [p. 462]. For Wasson [1969]:

> In the existential fictions of Sartre . . . the world of nature, of objects, of other people was always appropriated to the subjectivity of the hero and the author. The writers of the past did not accept the difference and distance between the subject and the Other, so they continually tried through metaphor to overcome continuities, to suggest through a reconciling metaphor a link between things. The process of metaphor . . . could only be accomplished by

incorporating the Contingent and the Other as symbols within one's own consciousness. [pp. 463–4]

Gerald Graff views, in his 1973 article *The Myth of the Postmodernist Breakthrough*, postmodernism as irrational because of its "rejection of the dominant academic tradition of analytic and interpretive criticism, which by reducing art to a set of intellectual abstractions tends to neutralize or domesticate its potentially liberating energies" [p. 384]. Therefore, it is a counterculture, which signifies a deep cultural crisis, or, more precisely, an ontological crisis that centers on a loss of consciousness of external reality, thereby an alienation from this reality and any reality whatsoever.

William Spanos comes close to Wasson since he regards history as an existential category, in terms of contingent events devoid of causality. He then discusses in detail the existential sources for postmodernism in a 1976 article titled *Heidegger, Kierkegaard, and the Hermeneutic Circle: Towards a Postmodern Theory of Interpretation as Dis-closure*. Spanos [1976] defines postmodernism as

> [A] hermeneutics which makes the interpreter a being-in-the-world in dialogic relationship simultaneously with a particular literary text and, since the text enters history on being written, with the "text" of literary history, and, beyond that, with the "text" of the history of Western man [sic]. [pp. 476–7]

Spanos's concern with history leads him to exclude the new novelists from the postmodern trend. Robbe-Grillet, for instance, focuses on literary form to break it out from world history and from human historicity.

The most significant among these theorists of postmodernism is Ihab Hassan. He was preoccupied with postmodernism for fifteen years, throughout which he published four manuscripts and numerous essays. In the beginning, he viewed postmodernism as anarchic, decreative, and antiformal [Hassan, 1981, p. 33] with antecedents such as Sade, Blake, and surrealism [p. 34–5]. However, as his thinking developed, he discerned the inadequacy of these features, since he added to them the desire to reveal a unified sensibility traversing limits, closing gaps, and realizing a new epistemic immediacy for the mind. Nevertheless, this episteme is governed by epistemological and ontological skepticism— hence, the difference between modernism and postmodernism. Whereas modernism created for itself forms of artistic authority, postmodernism tends toward artistic anarchy—therefore, decentralization. This decentralization leads to a postmodern world, which is marked by two characteristics: indeterminacy and immanence [or indetermanence]. "Indeterminacy" is a term that Ihab Hassan borrowed from Heisenberg's indeterminacy principle, which means for him the loss of ontological foundation—therefore, allowing for the emergence of forms of magic, Sufism [*Taṣawwuf* or Islamic mysticism], egolessness, and fragmentation. As for immanence, it is empty of any religious trace; by immanence, Hassan means the mind's ability to influence both the self and the world. With the absence of ontological centers, the human creates their self/ world, thanks to a language separate from the world of things. Consequently, immanence has a propensity for "oneness" [*al-tawḥīd*] and "globalization" [*al-kawkabeya*].

Amid this gamut of definitions of postmodernism, what remains?

Two sayings remain at the forefront: irrationality and misinterpretation. These two sayings do not diverge. Whoever stands against reason stands against interpretation. The mind, though a part of the world, transcends this world; whereas the mind is conscious of the world, the world is not self-conscious. In its consciousness of the world, the mind is not separate from it; therefore, it is an active participant co-constructing this world. This co-construction prevents us from seeing the world as it is in its truth. Consequently, it is not acceptable to say that the mind describes the world; rather what is acceptable is to say that the mind "interprets" the world, that is, it is not merely a "tabula rasa" that records the world's givens, but rather an active force. Accordingly, one can say that the conflict between modernism and postmodernism revolves around accepting or rejecting "interpretation."

If rejecting interpretation is a distinctive sign of postmodernism, then one can say that there is an organic relationship between postmodernism and religious fundamentalism to the extent that religious fundamentalism rejects interpreting the religious text because it adheres to its literality.

NOTES

Chapter 1

1 Zoroastrianism, Jainism, Shinto, Buddhism, Confucianism, Hinduism, Sikhism, Judaism, Christianity, Islam, and the Bahá'í Faith.

2 Tylor, E. B. (1871/2016). *Primitive culture: Researches into the development of mythology, philosophy, religion, language, art and custom* (1st ed.). Mineola, NY: Dover Publications, Inc.

3 Wahba, M. (1978). *The system in the philosophy of Bergson* (2nd ed.). Cairo, Egypt: Anglo-Egyptian Bookshop.

4 Empiricus, S. (1985). *Selections from the major writings on scepticism, man, & God* (S. G. Etheridge, Trans., 2nd ed., P. P. Hallie, Ed.). Indianapolis, IN: Hackett Publishing Company.

5 Ibn Rushd (Averroës). (1179/2012). *On the harmony of religion and philosophy* (G. F. Hourani, Trans.). Cambridge, UK: The E. J. W. Gibb Memorial Trust.

6 Ibid.

7 Locke, J. (1689). *A letter concerning toleration* (W. Popple, Trans.).

8 The word "fanatic" is derived from the Latin term *fanaticus*, which is derived from another Latin term *fanum*, that is, temple.

9 Al-Nashār, A. S. (1981). *Nash'at al-fikr al-falsafī fī al-Islām: Volume 1* (8th ed.). Cairo, Egypt: Dār al-Ma'ārif.

10 Burke, E. (1790/1951). *Reflections on the revolution in France*. London, UK: J. M. Dent & Sons Ltd.

11 Ibid.

12 Kirk, R. (1953/2001). *The conservative mind: From Burke to Eliot* (7th ed.). Washington, DC: Regnery Publishing, Inc.

13 Laws, C. L. (1920, July 1). Convention side lights. *Watchman-Examiner*. [New York].

14 Herbert, G. (1957). *Fundamentalism and the church of God* (pp. 18–19). London, UK: S.C.M. Press.

15 Ibid., pp. 20–21.

16 Viguerie, R. A. (1981). *The new right: We're ready to lead*. Falls Church, VA: Viguerie Co.

17 Ibid., pp. 151–61.

18 Ibid., p. 139.

19 Ibid., introduction.

20 The New Right is the Radical Right. The sociologist Seymour Martin Lipset coined the phrase "Radical Right" when he wrote about "the protection of traditional American values that characterizes 'status politics' as contrasted with the regard for jobs, cheap credit, or high farm prices, which have been the main emphasis of depression 'class politics'" [1955, p. 179]. For him, the practitioners of status politics are the Radical Right.

21 Viguerie, R. A. (1981). *The new right: We're ready to lead* (introduction). Falls Church, VA: Viguerie Co.

22 Bell, D. (Ed.). (1963). *The radical right: The new American right* (1st ed., pp. 304–41). Garden City, NY: Doubleday.

23 Maududi, S. A. A. (2000). The Political Theory of Islam. In Moaddel M., Talattof K. (eds.), *Modernist and fundamentalist debates in Islam* (pp. 263–71). New York, NY: Palgrave Macmillan.

24 Qutb, S. (1964/2006). *Milestones: Ma'alim fi'l-tareeq* (A. B. Al-Mehri Ed.). Birmingham, UK: Maktabah Booksellers and Publishers.

25 Ibid.

26 Shari'ati, A. (1979). *On the sociology of Islam: Lectures by Ali Shari'ati* (H. Algar, Trans.). Oneonta, NY: Mizan Press.

27 Antoun, R. T., & Hegland, M. E. (Eds.). (1987). *Religious resurgence: Contemporary cases in Islam, Christianity and Judaism*. Syracuse, NY: Syracuse University Press.

Chapter 2

1 Copernicus, N. (1543/1992). *On the revolutions of the heavenly spheres* (E. Rosen, Trans.). Baltimore, MD: The Johns Hopkins University Press.

2 Ibid, pp. 54–6.

3 Ibid, pp. 10–11.

4 Galilei, G. (1632/1967). *Dialogue concerning the two chief world systems: Ptolemaic and Copernican* (S. Drake, Trans., 2nd ed.). Berkeley, CA: University of California Press.

5 Becker, R. P. (Ed.). (1982). *German humanism and reformation: Erasmus, Luther, Muntzer, and others*. New York, NY: Continuum.

6 Zenkovsky, V. V. (1953). *A history of Russian philosophy: Volume I* (G. Kline, Trans.). Abingdon-on-Thames, UK: Routledge.

7 Kant, I. (1784/2009). *An answer to the question: "What is enlightenment?"* (H. B. Nisbet, Trans.). London, UK: Penguin.

8 Altizer, T. J., & Hamilton, W. (1966). *Radical theology and the death of God*. Indianapolis, IN: Bobbs-Merrill.

9 Berger, P. L. (1980). *The heretical imperative: Contemporary possibilities of religious affirmation* (1st ed.). Garden City, NY: Anchor Press.

Chapter 3

1 https://secularhumanism.org/a-secular-humanist-declaration/

Chapter 4

1 Bell, D. (1973). *The coming of post-industrial society: A venture in social forecasting*. New York, NY: Basic Books.

2 Fukuyama, F. (1989, Summer). The end of history? *The National Interest, 16*, 3–18.

3 Hegel, G. W. (1987). *Introduction to the lectures on the history of philosophy* (T. M. Knox, & A. V. Miller, Trans.). Oxford, UK: Clarendon Press.

4 Nietzsche, F. (1886/1990). Beyond good and evil: Prelude to a philosophy of the future (R. J. Hollingdale, Trans.). London, UK: Penguin.
5 Heidegger, M. (1947/1993). Letter on humanism. In D. F. Krell (ed.), *Basic writings: Ten key essays, plus the introduction to being and time*. San Francisco, CA: Harper.

REFERENCES

Al-Nashār, A. S. (1981). *Nash'at al-fikr al-falsafī fī al-Islām: Volume 1* (8th ed.). Cairo, Egypt: Dār al-Ma'ārif.

Altizer, T. J., & Hamilton, W. (1968). *Radical theology and the death of God*. Harmondsworth, UK: Penguin.

Antoun, R. T., & Hegland, M. E. (Eds.). (1987). *Religious resurgence: Contemporary cases in Islam, Christianity and Judaism*. Syracuse, NY: Syracuse University Press.

Arkoun, M. (1985). Islam et développement dans le Maghreb indépendant. In M. Wahba (ed.), *Future of Islamic civilization* (pp. 1–40). The Anglo-Egyptian Bookshop.

Bacon, F. (1620/2004). *Francis Bacon: The new organon* (L. Jardine & M. Silverthorne, Eds.). Cambridge, UK: Cambridge University Press.

Becker, R. P. (Ed.). (1982). *German humanism and reformation: Erasmus, Luther, Muntzer, and others*. New York, NY: Continuum.

Bell, D. (Ed.). (1963). *The radical right: The new American right* (1st ed.). Garden City, NY: Doubleday.

Bell, D. (1973). *The coming of post-industrial society: A venture in social forecasting*. New York, NY: Basic Books.

Berger, P. L. (1980). *The heretical imperative: Contemporary possibilities of religious affirmation* (1st ed.). Garden City, NY: Anchor Press.

Burggraff, D. L. (1995). Fundamentalism at the end of the twentieth century. *Calvary Baptist Theological Journal, 11*, 1–31. Retrieved from https://biblicalstudies.org.uk/pdf/cbtj/11-1_003.pdf

Burke, E. (1951). *Reflections on the revolution in France*. London, UK: J. M. Dent & Sons Ltd.

Callahan, D. (Ed.). (1966). *The secular city debate*. London, UK: Macmillan.

Copernicus, N. (1543/1992). *On the revolutions* (E. Rosen, Trans.). Baltimore, MD: John Hopkins University Press.

Council for Secular Humanism. (1980). A secular humanist declaration. Retrieved from https://secularhumanism.org/a-secular-humanist-declaration/

Cox, H. (1965). *The secular city: Secularism and urbanization in theological perspective*. London, UK: Macmillan.

Descartes, R. (1637/2006). *A discourse on the method: Of correctly conducting one's reason and seeking truth in the sciences* (I. Maclean, Trans.). Oxford, UK: OUP.

Drucker, P. F. (1993). *Post-capitalist society*. Abingdon-on-Thames, UK: Routledge.
Empiricus, S. (1985). *Selections from the major writings on scepticism, man, & God* (S. G. Etheridge, Trans., 2nd ed., P. P. Hallie Ed.). Indianapolis, IN: Hackett Publishing Company.
Fukuyama, F. (1989, Summer). The end of history? *The National Interest, 16*, 3–18.
Galilei, G. (1632/1967). *Dialogue concerning the two chief world systems: Ptolemaic and Copernican* (S. Drake, Trans., 2nd ed.). Berkeley, CA: University of California Press.
Graff, G. (1973). The myth of the postmodernist breakthrough. *TriQuarterly, 26*(4), 383–417.
Hassan, I. (1981). The question of postmodernism. *Performing Arts Journal, 6*(1), 30–37.
Hegel, G. W. (1892). *Lectures on the history of philosophy: Vol. I* (E. S. Haldane, Trans.). London, UK: K. Paul, Trench, Trübner, & Co., Ltd.
Heidegger, M. (1927/1962). *Being and time* (J. Macquarrie, & E. Robinson, Trans.). Oxford, UK: Blackwell.
Heidegger, M. (1947/1993). Letter on humanism. In D. F. Krell (Ed.), *Basic writings: Ten key essays, plus the introduction to being and time*. San Francisco, CA: HarperSanFrancisco.
Herbert, G. (1957). *Fundamentalism and the church of God*. London, UK: S.C.M. Press.
Howe, I. (1959). Mass society and post-modern fiction. *Partisan Review, 26*(3), 190–207.
Ibn Rushd (Averroes). (2012). *On the harmony of religion and philosophy* (G. F. Hourani, Trans.). Cambridge, UK: The E. J. W. Gibb Memorial Trust.
Kant, I. (1781/1998). *Critique of pure reason* (P. Guyer, & A. W. Wood, Trans.). Cambridge, UK: Cambridge University Press.
Kant, I. (1783/2004). *Kant's prolegomena to any future metaphysics* (G. Hatfield, Trans.). Cambridge, UK: Cambridge University Press.
Kant, I. (1784/2009). *An answer to the question: "What is enlightenment?"* (H. B. Nisbet, Trans.). London, UK: Penguin.
Kelman, H. C. (2005). The psychological impact of the Sadat visit on Israeli society. *Peace and Conflict, 11*(2), 111–136.
Khomeini, R. (1970). Islamic government: Governance of the jurist (H. Algar, Trans.). Institute for the compilation and Publication of Imam Khomeini's works.
Kirk, R. (2001). *The conservative mind: From Burke to Eliot* (7th ed.). Washington, DC: Regnery Publishing, Inc.
Köhler, M. (1977). "Postmodernismus": Ein begriffsgeschichtlicher Überblick. In *Amerikastudien/American Studies* (pp. 8–18). Stuttgart: JB Metzler.

Laws, C. L. (1920, July 1). Convention side lights. *Watchman-Examiner*. New York.

Levin, H. (1960). What was modernism?. *The Massachusetts Review*, *1*(4), 609–630.

Locke, J. (1989). *A letter concerning toleration* (W. Popple, Trans.).

Maududi, S. A. A. (1976/2000). The political theory of Islam. In: M. Moaddel, K. Talattof (eds.), *Modernist and fundamentalist debates in Islam* (pp. 263–71). London, UK: Palgrave Macmillan.

Nietzsche, F. (1886/1990). *Beyond good and evil: Prelude to a philosophy of the future* (R. J. Hollingdale, Ed.). London, UK: Penguin.

Nietzsche, F. (1887/2006). *Thus spoke Zarathustra* (A. D. Caro, & R. Pippin, Eds.). Cambridge, UK: Cambridge University Press.

Qutb, S. (2006). *Milestones: Ma'alim fi'l-tareeq* (A. B. Al-Mehri, Ed.). Birmingham, UK: Maktabah Booksellers and Publishers.

Shari'ati, A. (1979). *On the sociology of Islam: Lectures by Ali Shari'ati* (H. Algar, Trans.). Oneonta, NY: Mizan Press.

Sontag, S. (1966). *Against interpretation, and other essays*. New York, NY: Farrar, Straus & Giroux.

Spanos, W. V. (1976). Heidegger, Kierkegaard, and the hermeneutic circle: Towards a postmodern theory of interpretation as dis-closure. *Boundary*, *2*, 455–88.

Tylor, E. B. (1871/2016). *Primitive culture: Researches into the development of mythology, philosophy, religion, language, art and custom* (1st ed.). Mineola, NY: Dover Publications, Inc.

Viguerie, R. A. (1981). *The new right: We're ready to lead*. Falls Church, VA: Viguerie Co.

Wahba, M. (1978). *The system in the philosophy of Bergson* (2nd ed.). Cairo, Egypt: Anglo-Egyptian Bookshop.

Wahba, M. (1994). *Introduction to the enlightenment*. Cairo, Egypt: Dar al-'alam al-Thalith.

Wasson, R. (1969). Notes on a new sensibility. *Partisan Review*, *36*(3), 460–77.

Zenkovsky, V. V. (1953). *A history of Russian philosophy: Volume I* (G. Kline, Trans.). Abingdon-on-Thames, UK: Routledge.

PART II

ESSAYS

5

The Concept of the Good in Islamic Philosophy

In his book *Sufi Essays*, Nasr observes:

> Islam presents a view of life which is completely sacred and a freedom which begins with submission [to] the Divine Will.... [I]n the language of Islamic peoples there is no distinction between the sacred and the profane or temporal realm.... Through the Divine Law, which encompasses all human life, every human activity is given a transcendental dimension: it is made sacred and therefore meaningful. (Nasr, 1972, p. 166)

Once the Divine Law is established, of course, theology must be based upon it. Consequently, the arguments of the theologians involve nothing but quotations from the sacred texts. And these quotations provide the main evidence, sufficient and final, in terms of which any question is to be settled. The pivotal belief of most Islamic theologians is that *Allāh*'s Unity necessitates the dependence of all beings upon

Him. If this were not the case, there would be the possibility of transforming *Allāh* [God] into *ālihat* [gods]. In ethics, for example, if a person could judge what is good, they might overrule what *Allāh* rightly prescribes for them, and this would be blasphemous. This view is theistic, then, in that the decider of all values is taken to be *Allāh*.

In opposition to this generally held position stand the Muʿtazilites. Justice, according to them, is one of the attributes of *Allāh*, but it is a negative attribute, in the sense that *Allāh* does not commit acts that are evil and His acts cannot contradict human reason, which distinguishes between good and evil. Things, however, are either good or evil in themselves. Thus evil cannot be misidentified as the good, they contend, and the Divine Law cannot be against reason. It follows that reason is the basis of the idea of the good even prior to the Divine Law, and when the Divine Law appeared, it merely ensured what reason had said before. The Muʿtazilites also point out in this regard that if reason were unable to distinguish between good and evil, then the prophets would not have asked people to use their reason in distinguishing between them. The Divine Law itself, moreover, does not speak about the fine details of good and evil. These issues are left to human beings to work out with the aid of their reason. Given that they believe that reason perceives the moral value of acts, the Muʿtazilites consider this value—that is, the goodness or badness of the acts themselves—to be absolute. Thus *Allāh* does not determine, arbitrarily, the moral value of an act. On the contrary, this value is intrinsic in the act. All that *Allāh* does is inform us of this value through the revelation of the Prophet, if He finds that this information is necessary.

The most expressive figure among the Muʿtazilites is ʿAbd al-Jabbār. In his book *Summa on the Matters of Divine Unity and Divine Justice* [*Al-mughnī fī abwāb al-tawḥīd wa-l-ʿadl*], he states that good and evil are objective. In one sense, good is to be defined as nothing more than the negation of evil. But the absence of evil is still only a necessary, and not yet a sufficient, condition for good. This is evident from his classification of good acts. These are divided into three classes. The humblest class includes those acts for which the agent deserves neither blame nor praise for either doing them or not doing them. Among the examples he offers are breathing air and eating food. The next class of good acts includes those for which the agent deserves praise when they perform them, but for whose omission they do not yet deserve blame. Two kinds of acts fall into this class: those which do good directly to other people and those which induce a state of mind in which such acts will subsequently be done. To this there corresponds yet another distinction—between acts known as good by reason and those known as good by revelation. The third and last class is that of the obligatory act. According to al-Jabbār, an obligatory act is one for which a person capable of doing it deserves blame if it is not done.

Al-Ashʿarī and al-Ghazzālī argue against this line. Al-Ashʿarī emphasizes that we cannot be satisfied with reason if we are to discover how we are to act, for our moral principles can only stem from *Allāh*'s commands. Our knowledge of good and evil and of our duty is obtainable only through our acceptance of revelation, in which *Allāh* details the precise nature of His commands and prohibitions, in order that those who follow them may earn the enjoyment of rewards in the next life.

Al-Ghazzālī, on the other hand, objects to the idea of *Allāh* being confronted with human notions of good and evil, which have been given the status of an extrinsic and independent law. In arguing against the objectivity of ethics, then, al-Ghazzālī presents an explanation of how religious references can be incorporated into the meaning of ethical terms. He does this by interpreting the key ethical concepts of good and evil theologically. *Allāh*, he contends, is infinite. Thus it would be misleading to call any of His actions "good" in the normal sense. Consequently, His actions are not necessary but merely contingent. He could have acted otherwise. Al-Ghazzālī sums up his view as follows:

> We assert that it is admissible for God the exalted not to impose obligations on His servants, as well as to impose on them unachievable obligations to cause pain to His servants without compensation and without offense, that it is not necessary to Him to take notice of what is in their best interests, nor to reward obedience or punish disobedience and that it is not necessary for Him to send prophets, and if it is not necessary of God to send prophets and if He does not send them it is not evil or absurd, yet He is able to demonstrate their truthfulness by a miracle. (Sherif, 1975, p. 160)

This text implies that there is no point in arguing that *Allāh*'s actions are good since the notion of good is logically inappropriate as an attribute of divine action. Al-Ghazzālī denies, then, that independent reason is a sufficient guide to ethical knowledge, while the Mu'tazilites distinguish between two kinds of obligations: those that are known by reason alone and those that are known by revelation. By means of reason we can know the general direction in which moral activity must run, but by means of revelation we know the detailed rules that provide us with a practical guide to everyday actions. Against this claim, al-Ghazzālī argues as follows:

> In brief, whenever you wish to know the difference between those well-known judgments and the rational first principles, submit to your mind the statement "killing a human being is bad and saving him from death is good" after imagining that you have come into existence all of a sudden mature and rational, having, however, received no instruction, been associated with no community, experienced no human hierarchy or polity, but having simply experienced sensible objects. You would then be able to doubt these premises or at least hesitate in assenting to them, whereas you would be unable to experience such hesitation [in assenting to such claims as] "our statement's negation and affirmation are not true in one and the same state" and "two is greater than one."

Al-Ghazzālī then applies this principle to the discussion of goodness and badness. Human beings can only be servants of *Allāh*, he contends. Whether their service is good or bad depends upon the point of view adopted. From the viewpoint of *Allāh*, all actions are necessary and therefore good. But from the human viewpoint, the good may be described as pleasant, useful, or beautiful. The pleasant is felt immediately; the useful is judged from the perspective of ultimate ends; and the beautiful is gratifying at all times and in all situations. Bad things, by contrast, are those that are harmful. Just as things are *absolutely good* when they involve the three qualities of goodness—that is, utility, pleasure, and beauty—so things are *absolutely bad* when they involve all three qualities of evil—that is, harm, pain, and ugliness. In actuality, however, most things involve combinations of the above six qualities. Of the three qualities of the good, the most important is usefulness. And of those things that are useful, good deeds within faith are the most useful, for they serve the highest end of the human—their happiness.

After usefulness comes pleasure, in order of importance. Pleasures are either spiritual or bodily, but the first of these two categories is peculiar to the human. Accordingly, we can represent the hierarchy of the goodness of pleasures in the form of a pyramid. The base of this pyramid encompasses what all animals share, and as we move toward its apex, we hone in on what is peculiar to the human—which is to say, wisdom. Wisdom, being the pleasure of the spirit, is, of all the pleasures, the highest in the quality of its goodness, and wisdom in this sense refers to fellowship with *Allāh*.

The Islamic philosophers, however, were not all of one opinion concerning the nature of the good. According to Miskawayh, the good is the realization of the perfection of human existence. But humans differ in their disposition toward the realization of this end. Some are good by nature and, because their nature is unchangeable, they do not commit evil, but they are a minority. The majority is disposed toward evil. The third class is neither good nor evil and shifts from the evil to the good and vice versa through punishment or through accompanying the good humans.

The good is either general or particular, and there is absolute good, which is the Supreme Being. Good humans endeavor to grasp this Being. However, from the subjective viewpoint each individual has their own good and this is incarnated in their being conscious of happiness or pleasure. This particular good is nothing more than the emanation of acts from the individual in question, according to their essence. But as long as the individual is independent of others they are unable to realize these possible goods, and consequently individuals have to establish a community in which love for all humans is the basis of all virtues and duties. Hence the fruits of love flourish within and only within community, and asceticism and solitude are forbidden.

After Miskawayh comes al-Fārābī. At the beginning of his *Book of Letters* [*Kitāb al-ḥurūf*], al-Fārābī states that religion comes later in time than philosophy, since its aim is to teach the multitude theoretical and practical things that are deduced from philosophy in ways that facilitate the multitude's understanding. Theology and jurisprudence come later in time than religion and consequently are subordinate to it. Thus, according to this hierarchy, reason comes before revelation. In this sense al-Fārābī declares that reason is able to judge whether an act is good or evil. On this point he differs from the *Sunna* [i.e., normative precedents of the earliest Muslim community], who declare that the good is what *Allāh* orders and the evil is what *Allāh* has forbidden.

Al-Fārābī considers the good to be the perfection of Being, who at the same time is the Necessary Being. Evil, in turn, is the privation of this perfection. Given al-Fārābī's relating of the good to the Divine Being, so far as Providence encompasses all beings, it follows that they are all good. Therefore, the good is the substance of beings, and what seems to be evil in fact exists by accident. Thus it too can be considered good, even though it seems not to be. If you peer carefully into nature, you will find that many things, which seem to be catastrophic and evil, are, in reality, a means of destroying what is more evil and more dangerous. When human nature acts, however, good and evil definitely emerge. Thus al-Fārābī denies the reality of evil on the ontological level and affirms its existence on the moral level. And on this level, the exercise of will and choice determine one's orientation either toward good or toward evil, provided that the choice involved in the moral act is based on rational reasons. What are these rational reasons? They are derived from al-Fārābī's understanding of reason as being essentially political in nature. Thus he identifies the good with the political good, or justice, rather than the ethical good. The reasons underlying action within the moral realm, then, are political, which is why al-Fārābī is known primarily through his political writings—*The Virtuous City* [al-madina al-fadila], *The Political Regime* [al-siyāsa al-madaniyya], and *The Attainment of Happiness* [taḥṣīl al-saʿāda]. From these books it is evident that political science does not depend on the results of the investigation of beings above and beyond nature; rather, it builds on the foundations provided by natural science. It investigates those things by means of which the human reaches their perfection and distinguishes them from the things that obstruct their progress. It is concerned, that is to say, with the moral virtues and vices. Political science then considers the structure of the city and compares this to the structure of the world (excluding from this comparison any consideration of metaphysical or divine beings).

Accordingly, although the human is said to be a natural being and human science is said to belong to natural science rather than to metaphysics, political science is not reduced to natural science. The human is a natural being of a special kind, and the differences between the human and all other kinds of natural beings result from the difference in the way that nature prepares the human to achieve their perfection. It does not give the human their perfection but only the means for achieving it through will and choice. Unlike the other kinds of natural beings, the human is able to know the end toward which they must work as well as the means with which they are to perform the actions that bring them to that end. This knowledge is prior to, and the indispensable condition for, good action.

Thus, al-Fārābī states that reason alone can define what is good and what is evil, and the absolute good is the attainment of happiness. But this cannot be attained unless the human lives in political communities. It is impossible, in other words, for the isolated individual to attain the virtues conducive to the good human life. At the same time al-Fārābī emphasizes the fact that not all humans are capable of being virtuous. So a hierarchy is needed, because some individuals have no virtues, others have some virtues, and still others possess all virtues. These last are the philosophers, who must rule, while those without virtues or possessing only some virtues ought to be ruled and guided. For the rule of philosophy provides the only guarantee that those lacking in virtues may attain some semblance of well-being and happiness. In guiding them to happiness, the philosopher-ruler makes use of the Divine Law in order to promote in them virtues necessary for their happiness. They do this by means of a political act, which is lower than philosophy in rank and dignity, but superior to the Divine Law. This act is the establishment of the virtuous city, the existence of which is necessary for the well-being of the masses, but not for that of the philosophers, who may lead happy lives in an imperfect regime. The best city, according to al-Fārābī, is that which has been ruled by a series of virtuous kings. In view of the impossibility of establishing a perfect political city, however, the masses do well to live according to the rules of the Divine Law. The question now is: How does one make a community happy?

According to Ibn Sīnā, there is a relation between *Allāh* and goodness. *Allāh* is a necessary Being in essence as well as in all other aspects. That is, He could not be a Necessary Being in one sense and a contingent Being in another, because that would involve a contradiction. And if He is necessary and everything that is contingent has become possible by virtue of its necessity in Him, there remains nothing incomplete or lacking in Him to be explained—neither will, nor nature, nor knowledge, nor any of His attributes. Furthermore, He who is a Necessary Being in His essence is pure good and pure perfection. Thus the good is what every being keenly desires in order to perfect its existence. It is a condition of perfection and evil does not exist in essence. That is why Ibn Sīnā says, "Existence is goodness, and the perfection of existence is the goodness of existence." Thus a being that does not suffer any evil in the form of the absence of a substance, or of any undesirable state of it, is pure good. This could not apply to what is in essence a contingent being. As for goodness in the sense of the useful and profitable, this, of course, is only a matter of attaining perfection in things. *Allāh* contemplates His essence as well as the order of the good pervading all things. By doing so, that order emanates from Him to all existent things. We love and seek the good, but only for a purpose. *Allāh*, on the other hand, entertains no such purpose, and He possesses this form of pure intellectual will with no specific aim in view.

Evil, according to Ibn Sīnā, takes various forms. It may be a defect stemming from ignorance or from the disfigurement of the body; it may be something that causes pain or sorrow as the result of some act;

it may be just the lack of what brings happiness and provides for the good. In essence, it is the absence of something—a negative and not a positive element. It is not every form of negation but the nonexistence of what has been provided by nature for the perfection of things. Hence it is not something definite and determined in itself. If that were the case, there would exist what might be called "universal evil." As an accident, evil is the concomitant of matter and may come from outside and be an external factor, or from inside and be an internal factor.

To the question why *Allāh* did not make the pure good always prevail unaffected by the presence of evil, the answer is that such a situation would not be suitable for our genre of being. If we were to suppose the absence of evil, the consequences would constitute a still greater evil. Our judgment of evil is always relative and in terms of human action. It is with reference to something. Burning is for fire perfection and for those who may lose something as a result of it, an evil.

It should be observed that Ibn Sīnā offers no classification for an entity that destroys the essence of other entities, such as a positive theory of evil. Underlying his classification is his aim to establish the sense in which the Necessary Existent is the absolutely perfect. He specifies this feature of absolute perfection so as to stave off the objection that the emanation aspect of the Necessary Existent may lead to deficiency on Its part—a deficiency or loss of substance caused by the emanation of other entities from It. Accordingly, the Necessary Existent is portrayed as generating or sustaining goodness by being essential to the realization of other entities without losing anything in this process.

Good and evil are distinguished in the following ways: (1) with respect to the intention of the terms, differences are recognized between intrinsic goodness and instrumental goodness. (a) For example, something having intrinsic goodness may be good in itself if it leads to the perfection of some entities, which are imperfect, though these do not strive to accomplish such a good. (b) That which possesses instrumental goodness is a good by means of which other things become better. (2) Good and evil are further distinguished with respect to the extension of the terms. (a) We call that entity "totally good" from which nothing but good can come. (b) We call that entity "predominantly good" from which good may come even though evil exists within it. (c) Finally, we call that entity "predominantly evil" from which good may come even though evil is dominant within it. It is evident that in this context Ibn Sīnā wishes to identify the Necessary Existent with that which is intrinsically and predominantly good. It is also apparent that he has no classification covering totally evil entities.

Ibn Rushd (Averroës) follows al-Fārābī in focusing upon morality, not from the perspective of how it is to be acquired but in terms of how it is to be used to attain happiness. The question, once again, is about happiness and not about the good. As happiness is the end of the political community, there is no good per se, but only the good of either justice or happiness within the human will, and not within the Divine Will. In this sense, Ibn Rushd is opposed to the theologians who declare that what *Allāh* wills has no definite nature and merely turns on what the will of *Allāh* lays down for it. According to this argument, there is nothing good except by fiat. And more specifically, there is no end of the human other than by fiat. What brought them to this conclusion, of course, was a desire to defend the perfection of *Allāh*'s attributes, understood in terms of His capability of doing anything whatsoever. And by implication it follows that all things are in principle contingent. Ibn Rushd observes that these opinions of the theologians reflect the opinions of the multitude concerning the nature of ethics and in particular of the good. In these opinions, however, they are very far from a true understanding of the nature of the human and of the rational faculty, which distinguishes them from other beings. Through this specific nature the human is what they are and from this result the actions that are specific to them. This having been laid down, the good and the bad of a person's action are necessarily to be found only in the action specific to them. And this being the case, a person's end is attained only if they realize those of their actions that are specific to them in the utmost goodness. The good, instead of being theologized, has been secularized by Ibn Rushd, and this secularization of the good conforms to his observation in *The Decisive Treatise* [*fasl al-maqal*] that the sacred texts can be interpreted by human reason in such a way as to grasp the true meaning symbolized, whereas the theologians, and with them the masses, rest content with the apparent meaning for fear of employing their reason.

In this context, that is, in relation to their approach to scripture, Ibn Rushd classifies people into three classes. The first class is comprised of those who are not people of interpretation at all. These are the rhetorical class, and they constitute the overwhelming mass. The second class is comprised of the dialecticians. The third, or demonstrative, class is comprised of the people of certain interpretation. This interpretation, Ibn Rushd contends, is not to be expressed to the dialectical class, let alone to the masses. Accordingly, the concept of the good should be approached, as it is understood by the third class, if we want to grasp its human character.

One can say, then, that the concept of the good in Islamic philosophy has been secularized through Ibn Rushd's distinction of the three classes and his insistence that the masses are deprived of the ability to interpret which is the basis of secularization. This is evident from Ibn Rushd's definition of interpretation in *The Decisive Treatise*. He writes, "If the apparent meaning of Scripture conflicts with demonstrative conclusions, it must be interpreted allegorically, that is, metaphorically." He then expounds his famous definition of allegorical interpretation as "the extension of the significance of an expression from real to metaphorical significance." Thus Ibn Rushd claims that the scriptural texts have two meanings—an apparent meaning and a hidden one. The hidden meaning is disclosed by using human reason. Within this context the concept of the good can be conceived as a secular concept.

Having considered some of the ancient Islamic theologians and philosophers, we will now turn to the late nineteenth century and examine the thought of the most historical thinker, that is, Muḥammad 'Abduh, who was interested in determining the relation between revelation and reason in order to define the true ethical norms. In his *Treatise* [*risālat*], 'Abduh writes:

> The obligation to perform actions that are commanded or simply recommended, and to avoid or disapprove actions that are forbidden, in the manner prescribed by the Divine Law, which determines the appropriate rewards and penalties—all this reason cannot attain by itself. The only way to know, then, is by revelation.

> This is not to deny that what is commanded is already good in the sense that it leads to worldly or other-worldly benefit.

Thus revelation does not endow actions with the quality of goodness or evil, but only defines the obligation. What is commanded is "already good" for reasons that the human can understand. This means that reason can tell humans what they should or should not do and revelation gives them the most compelling reason why they should or should not do it. But since reason is often distorted in its operation by other human qualities, it seldom proves adequate even for its own primary role, and therefore most humans need the confirmation of revelation to help them decide what they should or should not do. Furthermore, although reason can provide reasons why one should behave in a certain way, these reasons lack compelling force, and therefore the religious imperative becomes necessary. This is evident from the following text:

> When have we ever heard that a class of people have made the good triumph in their actions solely on the grounds of the utility that this good offered for the masses or the elite, or that it prevented evil simply because it would have led to corruption and ruin? This has never occurred in human history and it is not in accord with human nature. The foundation of good habits rests only in dogmas and tradition, and these things themselves have no other basis than religion. Therefore, religion's power over men's minds is greater than the power of reason that is peculiar to them.

From this text we can conclude that the concept of the good has its roots in the Sacred Law and not in the secular law. In this sense, one could say that 'Abduh is the forerunner of the Muslim Brotherhood that was formed in Egypt by Hassan al-Banna in 1929. Its conception of goodness and evil was derived from 'Abduh's basic principle that the *Qur'ān* is the only source to which one can go for an identification of the good.

Bibliography

Writings

Averroës (1974). *Averroës on Plato's republic* (R. Lerner, Trans.). Ithaca: Cornell University Press.

Butterworth, C. E. (1986). *Philosophy, ethics and virtuous rule: A study of Averroës' commentary on Plato's "Republic."* Cairo: American University Press.

De Boer, T. J. (1984). *History of philosophy in Islam* (M. A. A. Ridah, Trans., 3rd ed.). Cairo: Committee of Translation and Publishing Press.

Hourani, G. F. (1971). *Islamic rationalism, the ethics of 'Abd Al-Jabbār*. Oxford: Clarendon Press.

Kerr, M. H. (1966). *Islamic reform, the political and legal theories of Mohammed 'Abduh and Rashid Rida*. Berkeley: University of California Press.

Sherif, M. A. (1975). *Ghazzali's theory of virtue*. Albany: State University of New York Press.

References & further reading

Afnan, S. M. (1958). *Avicenna, his life and works*. London: George Allen & Unwin.

Averroës (1960). *Averroës on the harmony of religion and philosophy* (G. F. Hourani, Trans.). London: Luzac.

Frank, R. M. (1978). *Beings and their attributes, the teaching of the Basrian school of the Mu'tazila in the classical period*. Albany: State University of New York Press.

Hourani, G. F. (1975). *Essays on Islamic philosophy and science*. Albany: State University of New York Press.
Leaman, O. (1995). *An Introduction to medieval Islamic philosophy*. Cambridge: Cambridge University Press.
Lerner, R., & Mahdi, M. (eds.) (1963). *Medieval political philosophy*. Ithaca: Cornell University Press.
Mahdi, M. (ed. and tr.) (1969). *Al-Fārābī's philosophy of Plato and Aristotle*. Ithaca: Cornell University Press.
Nasr, S. H. (1972). *Sufi essays*. London: George Allen and Unwin.
Nasr, S.H. (1978). *An introduction on Islamic cosmological doctrines*. London: Thames & Hudson.
Ridah, M. A. A. (ed.) (1978). *The philosophical treatises of Alkindi* (3rd ed.). Cairo: Dar Al Fikr Al Arabi.
Urvoy, Dominique (1991). *Ibn Rushd (Averroës)*. London: Routledge.

6

Philosophy in North Africa

In *The Rise and Fall of the Roman Empire*, Gibbon describes the tragic end of Hypatia, the female Egyptian philosopher of antiquity. She taught Greek philosophy and found that there is no contradiction between Neoplatonism and Christianity. From this standpoint, she adopted Nestorius's theory of Christ as having two natures, the divine and the human, loosely united. At that time Nestorius, as a result of this theory, was condemned at the council of Ephesus in 431 and was declared a heretic. Hypatia was, accordingly, execrated as a follower of a heretic, and in 415 she was killed in an unspeakably gruesome manner by some monks in an assassination endorsed by Cyril, patriarch of Alexandria.

In a nutshell, one can say that the second half of the fifth century was the end of philosophy in Egypt. But in Europe, in the eighteenth century, during the Age of Enlightenment, Hypatia appeared for the first time as a cause célèbre in religious and philosophical polemics. In 1720, John Toland published a long historical essay titled *Hypatia* in which he focused on the patriarch Cyril, who was the contriver of so horrid a deed as the murder of Hypatia, and his Alexandrian clergy, who were the executors of his implacable fury. Voltaire used the figure of Hypatia to express his repugnance for the church and revealed religion. In his view, Hypatia was murdered because she believed in rational thinking and trusted the capacities of the human mind freed of imposed dogma (see Dzielska 1995, pp. 109–10). That comment was made in the eighteenth century. In the twentieth century, Bertrand Russell, quoting Gibbon's description of the murder of Hypatia, comments wryly that after it Alexandria "was no longer troubled by philosophers" (1946, p. 368).

In 1198, an even more dramatic incident took place in Córdoba, Spain, in which the Islamic philosopher Ibn Rushd was accused of being an atheist. His books were burnt and he was banished to Lucena. The reason for this persecution was his concept of interpretation. He writes:

If the apparent meaning of Scripture conflicts with demonstrative conclusions it must be interpreted allegorically, i.e., metaphorically. This being so, whenever demonstrative study leads to any manner of knowledge about any being, that being is inevitably either unmentioned or mentioned in Scripture. If it is unmentioned there is no contradiction and it is in this case an act whose category is unmentioned, so that the lawyer has to infer it by reasoning from Scripture. If Scripture speaks about it, the apparent meaning of the words inevitably either accords or conflicts with the conclusions of demonstrations about it. If this apparent meaning accords there is no argument. If it conflicts there is a call for allegorical interpretation of it. The meaning of allegorical interpretation is:

extension of significance of expression from real to metaphorical significance.

The reason why I think that this definition of the term "interpretation" is the explanation for the persecution of Ibn Rushd is that it legalizes diversity of interpretation and, consequently, eliminates the illusion of Absolute Truth; obviously, if this illusion is negated, then no one has the right to charge another of unbelief and, hence, *ijmā'* (consensus) and its concomitant dogmatism is also negated. Consequently, Ibn Rushd has been marginalized in Islamic culture or, strictly speaking, neglected. On the other hand, in Europe his books were translated into Latin and Hebrew in the thirteenth century following the political decision of Emperor Frederick II. Frederick made this decision having grown up in a society where a new culture—that is, a secular culture—was in the making. Hence, Ibn Rushd's philosophy played a decisive role in the emergence of two complementary movements.

The first movement was the Reformation led by Luther, with his motto "Free inquiry into the Scripture." This motto is analogous to Ibn Rushd's statement (1976, p. 53) that unanimity cannot be established in the interpretation of the *Qur'ān*. Both Luther and Ibn Rushd were accused of being heretics for holding basically the same position. Jean de Jandun of France (1275–1328), who politically opposed the papacy, claimed that there is no principle of belief except reason and experience. He supported the doctrine of the distinctness of the philosophical and religious levels of discourse that was adopted by the Latin Averroists in the fourteenth century. His political collaborator, Marsile de Padou, drew a distinction between reason and faith, the temporal and the spiritual, the church and the state, in the domain of politics. In terms of this distinction, he maintained that the basis of politics should be secular and not religious.

The second movement was the Enlightenment, which is considered the age of reason or the sovereignty of reason. The writers of the mid-eighteenth century challenged the views of history and human nature as well as of the universe that were endorsed by the Church of Rome. Kant is considered the philosopher who summed up the achievements of the Enlightenment. In his *Critique of Practical Reason*, moral duty was withdrawn from possible determination by the material world of perceived phenomena. This implied a refusal to subordinate moral duty to the authorities of the world. The concept of a social contract was adopted as a doctrinal counterbalance to the theory of the divine right of kings. It was adopted to show the sovereignty of reason as the ultimate source of moral authority. Ibn Rushd was the forerunner of this point of view.

But the propagation of the ideas of these two movements was not an easy task for the Averroists. They faced a severe struggle, especially in the European universities. Albert the Great published a book titled *Unity of Intellect Against Averroists* and Thomas Aquinas wrote *Contra Averroistas*. Thus Averroism was condemned in 1265 as a heresy. In December 1270, the bishop of Paris, Etienne Tempier, condemned fifteen doctrines, thirteen of them were of Averroist inspiration. Here I mention only the doctrines concerning the mortality of the soul, the unity of the active intellect, and the negation of divine providence.

Now, what happened in the Arab world with respect to Ibn Rushd? As previously mentioned, he was totally rejected, even by Muslim reformists such as Muḥammad ʿAbduh. The Islamic thinkers objected to the secularization that was one of the important features of Ibn

Rushd's rationalism. This opposition was, in fact, an echo of the collective reaction in the Arab world that may be classified into three types: traditionalism, abortive modernism, and moderate modernity.

Traditionalism is to be viewed as a negative attitude toward Western civilization and toward any futuristic outlook, on the grounds that the locus of the Golden Age was the past and not the future. Abortive modernism is to be understood as a positive attitude toward the West, but it is at the same time tradition-bound. It is not much more than what one might call an enlightened traditionalism. And that is why abortive modernism, in its fundamental premises and ultimate conclusions, opposes the secular elements of social modernization even more effectively than traditionalism. Moderate modernity may be regarded as a proposed remedy for the previous two conditions of the mind. It sought to interpret tradition within a secular framework free from cultural taboos.

The two most influential figures in the traditionalist movement were Jamāl al-Dīn al-Afghānī (1839–97) and Muḥammad 'Abduh (1849–1905). It must be stressed from the start that this movement, spearheaded by these two Muslim thinkers, did not question Islamic dogma. Its primary motivation was to meet the challenge the West posed to the Arab world by strengthening Islamic dogma rather than exposing it to rational criticism.

Al-Afghānī put the issue of the decadence of Islam in clear and terse words, "Every Muslim is sick, and his only remedy is in the Qur'ān" (1995). Thus, the problem of the Muslim world was not how to be strong but how to understand religion and live in accordance with its teachings. Pursuing this theme, al-Afghānī published a book titled *The Refutation of the Materialists* [*al-radd 'alā al-dahrīyīn*], which became the model for traditionalist thought. Those he attacked under the name of materialists included virtually all, from Democritus to Darwin, together with all those in Islam who gave an explanation of the world without invoking the existence of a transcendent *Allāh*. Al-Afghānī's preoccupation with Western materialism reflected a general Muslim bias against science, which was regarded as responsible for the disintegration of traditional Christianity and which was now threatening Islam. It is, therefore, not surprising that this stance blocked logically oriented discourses and contributed to deflecting interest in rational criticism.

Thus, al-Afghānī formulated the general direction of traditionalism, but it was 'Abduh who, using al-Afghānī's teachings as a springboard, gave it its precise formulation. The task he set himself involved two things: first, a restatement of what Islam really was; second, a consideration of its implications for modern society. Regarding the first point, 'Abduh was of the opinion that reason must accept everything that is in the *Qur'ān* without hesitation. Once reason acknowledges that Muḥammad was a prophet, it must accept the entire content of his prophetic message. The second point proceeds from the first. If reason is controlled by the *Qur'ān*, then the ideal society will have to be granted to be that which submits to *Allāh*'s commandments, since these commandments are also the principles for the well-ordering of human society. The behavior that the *Qur'ān* teaches to be pleasing to *Allāh* is also that which modern social thought must teach as the key to progress. Islam is the true sociology, the science of happiness in this world as well as in the next. So when Islamic law is fully obeyed, society flourishes; and when it is rejected, society decays.

For 'Abduh, this is not just the ideal society but also one that once actually existed. His imagination is fixated on the golden age of Islam and that is why he was against secular society. One proof of this fact is the dispute between 'Abduh and Farah Antun on the occasion of a book published by the latter in 1903 on the life and philosophy of Ibn Rushd. In his dedication, Antun declares that the book is meant for "the new shoots of the East," by which he meant "those men [and women] of sense in every community and every religion of the east" who have seen the danger of mingling the ordinary affairs of the world with religion in an age like ours, and have realized the necessity of moving "with the tide of the European civilization, in order to be able to compete with those who belong to it, for otherwise it will sweep them all away and make them the subjects of others" (1903, p. 3).

A little further on, Antun explains why he writes about Ibn Rushd: it is to separate temporal from religious authority. There are five reasons why this is necessary. The most important is the third one in which he states that since the religious authorities legislate with a view to the next world, their control would interfere with the purpose of government, which is to legislate for this world. Implicit in this reason lies the presupposition that the State must be neutral toward all religions and hence tolerant. This was in direct opposition to 'Abduh's belief for two reasons. First, for 'Abduh, the separation of religion and the State was not only undesirable but also impossible, for the ruler must belong to a specific religion. Second, he maintained that if religion is purified, it could be the basis of political life. Antun's reply was that states are no longer based on religion but on national unity as well as modern science and technology. But 'Abduh's philosophy prevailed with the rise of the Muslim Brotherhood, headed by Hassan al-Banna (1906–49), the initiator of Islamic fundamentalism in Egypt in the 1940s.

We come now to the second movement, that is, abortive modernism. The most influential figures are Yūsuf Karam (1886–1959, Egypt), Othman Amin (1905–87, Egypt), Zaki Naguib Mahmoud (1905–93, Egypt), Abdel-Rahman Badawi (1917–2002, Egypt), Malek Bennabi (1905–73, Algeria), Mohammed Aziz Lahbabi (1923–93, Morocco). We begin with Yūsuf Karam, the advocate of moderate rationalism. He wrote the history of Greek, medieval, and modern philosophy, commenting on every philosophical system, either supporting or rejecting it, on the basis of his own system of "moderate rationalism," which is propagated in his two books *Reason and Existence* [*al-'aql wa-al-wujūd*] as well as *Physics and Metaphysics* [*al-ṭabī'ah wa-mā ba'da al-ṭabī'ah*].

Karam's "moderate rationalism" reflects the influence of the neo-Thomism that was advocated by Jacques Maritain, under whom Karam studied philosophy at the Catholic Institute in France at the beginning of the First World War. According to Karam's system, the mind can strive toward truth and, thus, can attain certainty. Through its capacity for abstraction, which is the mediator between mind and object, the mind attains to the essence of things. It is this mediation that guarantees scientific objectivity. Karam, therefore, is against the sensualists, because they exclude reason and believe only in the senses. But he is also against those rationalists who deny abstraction, since they fail to locate the real cause that relates the mind to objects.

Abstraction also provides a justification for metaphysics. Due to abstraction, the mind is able to transcend sensible nature to her non-sensible origins and conditions and is thus able to grasp existence per se, which is the subject of metaphysics. Justifying this science in this manner leads Karam to investigations that result in proofs of the immortality of the soul and the existence of *Allāh*.

The immortality of the soul rests on three proofs. The first is a metaphysical proof, which holds that the human soul is independent of the body in its existence and in its exercise of the mind and the will. The soul, therefore, is immortal and is not annihilated with the extinction of the body. The second is a psychological proof, derived from the basic natural inclination toward eternal survival. And the third is a moral proof resulting from the necessity of final and total sanctions for our free actions. Such sanctions necessitate another life, since they cannot be realized in nature because it is non-mortal. Neither can they be realized in society because society deals only with our outward actions, nor by the conscience because it cannot judge itself. For the existence of *Allāh*, there were plenty of proofs. The most important of these, according to Karam, are the following three: the proof from motion to an unmoved mover, from the fact of order to the existence of its designer, and from the contingent to the necessary. The third argument, like the first, depends upon the principle of causality and is formulated in the statement: "There is a cause for everything that exists." The second relies upon the principle of teleology and is formulated in the statement: "Every action must have a purpose." Karam argues that the principles of causality and teleology are a priori principles of the mind. Such principles are universal because they are presupposed by the existence of the mind and perception.

For Karam, the function of the mind is judgment, not action, which pertains to the will. As to the question of the relation between the mind and the will, Karam's answer is that each is a cause that is in some way related to judgment. However, they differ in that the will is the *cause efficace* of the mind's activity in judgment because it directs the mind in a direction. The judgment of the mind is the *cause finale* of the will because it offers to the will a specific cause. The direction of the mind by the will forestalls the clash between the mind and religion, since it is the will rather than the mind that fosters faith. Karam writes: "If a person's behavior is straight and firm, their will is ready for faith, and it will direct the mind towards finding support for this belief." The significance of this statement is that the mind per se neither accepts nor refuses belief. That is, it does not gravitate toward a specific belief. The mind is directed toward a specific belief by accepting external reasons under the influence of the will. The inevitable consequence of this "moderate rationalism" is that faith is beyond reason.

Othman Amin (1964) is the advocate of the "Philosophy of Inwardness" (*al-Gouwania*). It is a philosophy that tries to see people and things from a spiritual angle. In other words, it tries to see the invisible world by not limiting itself to the visible. It seeks the inward being, not stopping at the outward. Many traditions, traced to the Prophet Muḥammad, emphasize this opposition between the invisible and the visible. For example: "God does not look at your face and wealth, but at your heart and your actions" (Amin, 1964). In this religious sense, *al-Gouwania* is a synonym for freedom. Freedom must not be sought in the possession of objects, like wealth and honors, but in the soul, that is, in something of absolute autonomy, namely, faith in *Allāh* and attachment to human dignity. In this sense, Amin thinks that he is combining Western philosophy with the framework of the Islamic tradition. He says: "I now go back to the philosophical explanation of *al-Gouwania*. In this respect Maine de Biran is of great help. He says that there is much difference between knowing a truth through our intelligence and having it always present in our soul" (Amin, 1964). Later on he states that the philosophy of *al-Gouwania* adopts the distinction made by Bergson between two very different ways of knowing: "the one being the way of inward vision, penetration by the spirit, by intellectual sympathy; the other the way of exterior vision, effected by using the testimony of the senses or by applying logical analysis alone."

Concerning his concept of freedom, Amin assumes that it is found in Cartesian ethics, which aims at establishing the mastery of the soul over the passions, and in Kant's idea of the moral law, which is wholly inward and a priori, that is to say, preceding and conditioning all experience and not being derived from the exterior world.

Because of his idealist tendencies, Amin is against logical positivism and historical materialism. He is against logical positivism because, in his view, it stops at the limits of the senses and the experimental method and, therefore, denies the capabilities of reason; furthermore, he is against historical materialism on the grounds that it uses science to abolish the human and, consequently, religion since the human, according to Amin's definition, is a religious animal.

The consequence of this is that Amin approaches social issues not only in an idealist manner but also in a religious manner. He uses the question of socialism as an example of this double approach. According to him, the idealist approach regards the notion of socialism, above all, as an Absolute Truth that exists in the mind in the form of an impersonal existence, unlimited neither by time nor by space. In the religious approach, neither the nontemporal nor the nonspatial can serve as a theory or ideology, nor can they be subject to any law, but can only serve as a subject of religious faith. Therefore, socialism has to be Islamic socialism, and its pioneers are Jamāl al-Dīn al-Afghānī, Muḥammad ʿAbduh, Abd al-Rahman al-Kawakibi (1855–1902, Syria), and Muḥammad Iqbal (1877–1938, Pakistan), because they awakened the socialist consciousness of the society.

The purpose of such a philosophical system, according to its advocate, is to restore to our atomic age and to the age of historical materialism and logical positivism, faith in *Allāh*, and allegiance to the human. However, in all the lectures he delivered at Cairo University in the late 1950s, Amin harshly criticized logical positivism more than historical materialism. This can be explained by the fact that Zaki Naguib Mahmoud, who was a professor of philosophy in the same department, adhered to logical positivism.

Zaki Naguib Mahmoud adopts the attitude of logical positivism toward science. Science, for him, is natural, experimental science, and the basis of scientific knowledge is constituted by the senses, which are the only source of knowledge. The scientific outlook obliges us not to deviate from ascertainable facts. Since basing our investigations on data arising from reality, as ascertained through sense experience, is the only legitimate methodology of scientific research, the scientific outlook leads to positivism. If the data that preoccupy the researcher are of a linguistic character, dealing with the structure and relationships of statements, positivism in that case becomes "logical." Hence, the label "logical positivists" denotes a group of thinkers who do not accept that there can be any reality transcending sense experience and who concern themselves with the structure and significance of the language of science. Hence, philosophy should be limited to the linguistic analysis of scientific statements.

Zaki Naguib Mahmoud (1955) reaches two important conclusions through his linguistic analysis. The first is that the logical analysis of mathematical sentences indicates that they are tautologies, and that their certainty is due to the fact that they say nothing. He writes: "This strange discovery about the nature of the mathematical sentence justifies the contention that there is only one source of knowledge for man [sic], namely, the senses and that nothing can justify an element of belief beyond the senses, and deriving from an independent faculty, such as the mind." The second conclusion is that value "is purely a subjective expression which has nothing to do with the external world." The significance of this is that if two people disagree about a value judgment, "the only alternative would be to resort to an external criterion to decide who is wrong and who is right."

The question now is: What is Zaki Naguib Mahmoud's motivation for adopting this interpretation of science? The motivation is a social one. In one of his later books (Mahmoud, 1971), he says that his aim is to reconcile the Arab tradition with modernism. But what does he mean by "the Arab tradition"? According to him, it is the configuration of techniques by which our ancestors lived. Our task then is to choose the techniques that can help us in our contemporary living. Hence, the Arab tradition is not a matter of ideology but of technology.

What of modernism? According to Mahmoud, "Logical positivism represents the spirit of modernism." That is why it is an essential part of his philosophy to affirm a distinction between factual judgment and value judgment; the former is scientific, the latter is not. As a consequence, one cannot speak of a scientific approach to the study of social change, since this is essentially a matter of values. Hence, ideology is also nonscientific, and it is nonsense to talk of an ideological struggle. That is why, according to Mahmoud, the terms "capitalist society" or "socialist society" are to be replaced with "technological society" or "post-industrial society."

This conception has defined the main tendency in modern bourgeois ideology, and it has received the name of "de-ideologization," which is an attempt to propagate an apolitical state of mind that does not care either for social change or for society. That is why Mahmoud is consistent in his philosophy when he writes, "Owing to my philosophical position, I approve of anything that can strengthen the individuality of the individual and that can destroy society in case solidarity were to grow at my own expense. There is no real fact except my own being, and everything else is but an instrument for strengthening this being" (1955, p. 10). This statement confirms our point of view that de-ideologization is an ideological weapon used against social change.

Abdel-Rahman Badawi comes to the same conclusion but through atheistic existentialism. According to him, existence and time are synonymous. In his book *Existential Time* [*al-zaman al-wujudi*], he declares that any existence that is not temporalized is an absolute impossibility. Since time, for Badawi, is divided into physical and subjective time, there is, likewise, physical and subjective existence. Physical existence is the existence of objects in the world in which the human exists, while subjective existence is the existence of the self as an independent and quite isolated being. Consequently, communication between selves is initially totally absent. However, this chasm may be overcome by means of a certain kind of leap. But this leap cannot be explained rationally, according to Badawi. The reason is that nothingness is an essential factor in the structure of existence, and the irrational is the intellectual expression of existential nothingness. Modern physics, he argued, corroborates the notion of the irrational. The indeterminism of quantum theory and wave mechanics is quite irrational in the sense that it cannot be reduced to a purely rational system. In this matter, Badawi relies on Louis de Broglie's assumption that physics should reject the idea of causal continuity and limit itself to deducing laws, which are necessarily of a statistical nature.

Badawi held also that self-knowledge cannot be attained by reason but by another faculty, namely, intuition. The logic of intuition is tension. This tension means the inability to resolve a contradiction. And this is the meaning of the dialectic, which functions only within the self and not outside of it.

Badawi considers his system an appropriate ideology for Arab society. In an article published in 1967, he argues in justification for his claim by appealing to the Islamic heritage as represented in Sufism. He finds a close connection between Sufism and existentialism. Both start from subjectivism and place subjective existence above physical existence. The purpose of discipline in Sufism is to release the self from external encumbrances so that the self can be left alone to develop. The notion of the perfect human for the Sufis means a self-realization that is possible only in the human. In this way, humanity becomes a substitute for *Allāh*. But such humanity is a subjective, rather than an objective, humanity.

The main theme of the Algerian philosopher Malek Bennabi is the reconstruction of Islamic society so that it can be free from exploitation and imperialism and capable of coping with modern civilization. This is impossible, Bennabi maintains, unless the Islamic idea becomes efficient. By efficient, he means being able to change the world radically to create history. He says that this kind of efficiency was realized during the Prophet's time in the creation of the Islamic Empire and the establishment of Islamic Truth. One might object that truth should not be identified with one point of view but many. Although this objection might be well taken from Bennabi's standpoint, he insisted that no one could deny the efficiency that was achieved during the period in question.

What does this mean, according to Bennabi? It means that truth is subjective, while efficiency is objective. Hence, objective factors are required for the realization of efficiency. Unfortunately, these conditions are absent nowadays for two reasons: the presence of imperialism and the absence of ideas. The first reason is obvious, but the second one is obscure and has to be explained in detail. According to Bennabi's theory, there are three worlds that are necessary for any civilization: the world of ideas, the world of persons, and the world of things. The leading world is the world of ideas because the human is distinguished from the nonhuman animal by reason, and this means that our idea of a thing precedes its realization in reality. Therefore, ideas have the ability to change the world of persons and the world of things.

Here, the question may be raised: What is the matter with the world of ideas in the Islamic world at the present time? Bennabi's answer is that the world of ideas is absent, and its absence is due to two factors: the first is objective, and the second is subjective. According to Bennabi, imperialism is the objective factor. It negates the creative powers of the human by involving them in the world of things instead of ideas. In this way, the human regresses to the infantile stage, which is characterized by handling things without knowing what they are. That is why imperialism is always keen to sell us things rather than ideas. Even when it does sell us ideas, it sells them only after distorting and falsifying them. But, as an objective factor, imperialism would be ineffective without the subjective factor, which is the susceptibility to imperialism on the part of the victim. This susceptibility is seen in the inability to utilize one's potentialities for raising one's standard of living. Bennabi (1970) argues further that liberation from imperialism implies liberation from the susceptibility toward capitalism. Hence, any revolution neglecting this subjective factor condemns itself to failure.

But how could a revolution avoid such failure? Through a cultural revolution, replies Bennabi. It turns out, however, that such a revolution is put forward as a necessary but not sufficient condition. To achieve efficiency through the Islamic idea, there is also the need for an "explosive economic policy" to liberate the productive forces. But what is the definition of this technical term: "explosive economic policy?" Bennabi's definition is that it is neither the capitalist pattern nor the Marxist pattern. But what is it specifically? We get no answer from Bennabi, and this is his dilemma, for one cannot control and orientate social change if one lacks a clear idea of what is required for such a change.

I come now to Lahbabi. He gives a radical analysis of the decadence of the Muslim world in light of the original fountains of Islam, that is, the *Qur'ān* and the *Sunnah*. On that basis, he calls for a sweeping transformation of the status quo and the attitudes allied to it, which are extremely backward. He advocates going back to original Islam and shedding off all blind faith in holy texts or *taqlīd* [following established legal precedents] and insists on an *ijtihād* [legal reasoning], that is, a rethinking for oneself of the meaning of the original message. In light of this conception of Islamic revivalism (*Salafiyya*), Lahbabi outlines what he takes to be the radical difference between the *Salafiyya* and the Western Renaissance.

The Renaissance in the West was, according to Lahbabi, a rupture in the continuity of the given civilization. One was freed from the medieval style of thinking to enslave oneself in the ways of antiquity, thus instantiating the tactic of taking one step forward and two steps backward. On the other hand, the *Salafiyya* goes back to the sources of Islam without rejecting any fresh cultural acquisitions, whether Islamic or not. There is a going back to the *Qur'ān* and the *Sunnah* to liberate the dogma and the laws from superstition. The *Salafiyya* is a search for the original force of Islam. It is a creative going back, whereas the Renaissance was a reaction against the Middle Ages. By means of a paradoxical process, progress is realized through reaction, through the imitation of the thought of the Greeks and Romans. For the Muslims, by contrast, the Middle Ages were a time of creativity and of free interpretation in all fields. In this sense, one might say that a marriage was struck between the sacred and the secular. The classics of Greek antiquity, especially in philosophy and the sciences, were taken not as perfect models, as they were during the Renaissance, but as something that could be adapted.

But in my opinion, Lahbabi's theory suffers from two weaknesses. The first is that he does not fully elaborate a specific method; the second is that he does not tackle the social implications of his thesis. Thus, it is noticeable that Lahbabi has not been able to subdue the ever-haunting ghost of the West. Certainly, the medieval religious output of Muslims cannot provide us today or tomorrow with any intelligible guidance, even though there is much that is highly valuable in this medieval body of thought.

This is why Lahbabi is right when he assumes that the weakness of the Arab intellectuals is their confinement to two approaches, the traditionalist (*Salafi*) and the eclectic. Together, these tendencies have the effect of abolishing the historical dimension. But ahistorical thinking has but one consequence: failure to see the Real. The only way to transcend these two modes of thought consists in strict submission to the discipline of historical thought and the acceptance of its presuppositions. These presuppositions include the existence of the laws of historical development, the unity of the meaning of history, and the effectiveness of the political role of the philosopher. But the *Salafi* does not accept these presuppositions, they believe in Providence and the eclectics are, consequently, at the mercy of every passing fashion. But, in my opinion, it is not easy to adopt historical thinking, which requires a certain stage of civilizational development that is exemplified by the Enlightenment—namely, the liberation of human reason from any authority except reason itself.

As for the third type of orientation in modern Islamic philosophy, namely moderate modernity, its representative figures are Mohammed Arkoun (1928–2010, Algeria) and Mohammed Abed al-Jabri (1935–2010, Morocco). Arkoun claims that there are two kinds of text, the oral and the written, which is the *Qurʾān*. But this written text has nothing to do with revelation. The sacred language is liable to be secularized. If this is done quietly, there is no trouble. On the other hand, this same sacred text might be transformed into orthodoxy. When that happens, any thinker who tries to secularize it will be accused of being an apostate and a destroyer of the political system. In the latter situation, it might seem as if religion rules. But if we dig deeper, we find that religion does not really rule and that the ruler does not actually yield to *Allāh* either. What happens, one might ask, if we are late to digging even deeper? In that case we may be deceived into thinking that our beliefs are not open to argument. Accordingly, we may wallow in the imaginary beliefs embedded in religious language and rituals.

Thus, according to Arkoun (1993), we have, on the face of it, two types of reason: the dogmatic and the secular. But our task is to fuse the one with the other so as to eliminate the false dichotomy. In this way, we could establish what Arkoun calls Islamic humanism with a secular flavor. This kind of Islam was aborted in the eleventh century on the pretense that Islam is against secularization due to cultural taboos. However, in defense of his thesis, Arkoun argues that secularization, in fact, emerged in the year 661, that is, within thirty years of the death of Prophet Muḥammad. Thus, true secularization is not opposed to religion per se.

As for al-Jabri (1991), he is engaged in the analysis of the Arab mind within the tradition of *taqlīd*. Hence, he tackles the problem of modernity and authenticity for the sake of a Renaissance project that can and will confront backwardness. The problem, he finds, is that Islamic culture is unable to produce new things and hence displays little creativity. This means that the contemporary Arab milieu is synonymous with tradition. The paradox here, according to al-Jabri, is that the Arabs are the only people on Earth whose tradition is contemporaneous with their contemporary thought.

References

'Abduh, Muḥammad (1931). *Kharitat Jamal al-Din al-Afghānī al-Husayni* (Thoughts of Jamal al-Din al-Afghānī al-Husayni). Beirut: Dar Al Kindi.

Al-Afghānī, Jamal el-Din (1995). *The refutation of the materialists* (M. 'Abduh, Trans., 2nd ed.). Cairo: Al-Halabi.

Al-Jabri, M. (1991). *Tradition and modernity*. Morocco: The Center for Arab Unity Studies.

Amin, Othman (1964). *Al-Gouwania or the philosophy of inwardness*. Cairo: Dar al Kalam.

Antun, Farah (1903). *Ibn Rushd and his philosophy*. Cairo: The University.

Arkoun, M. (1993). *Secularization and religion*. Dar el-Saki.

Averroës (Ibn Rushd) (1976). *The decisive treatment* (G. Hourani, Trans.). London.

Bennabi, Malek (1970). *Vocation of Islam*. Beirut: Dar El Fikr.

Dzielska, M. (1995). *Hypatia of Alexandria*. New York: Harvard University Press.

Lahbabi, A. (1967). *Le Persalisme Musulman*. Paris: PUF.

Mahmoud, Zaki Naguib (1955). *Days in America*. Cairo: The Anglo Egyptian Bookshop.

Mahmoud, Zaki Naguib (1971). *Revival of Arab thought*. Beirut: Dar Al Sherouk.

Russell, B. (1946). *History of western philosophy*. London: Allen and Unwin.

INDEX

'Abduh   64, 67, 116–18, 123–6, 131
Absolute Truth   vii, xvi, xxi, xxiv, 7–14, 47, 122, 130
Al-Fārābī   5, 10, 109–11, 114
Allāh   xxviii, 12–13, 31–3, 41, 59, 61, 70–1, 73–6, 103–9, 112–15, 125, 128–9, 131, 134, 139
Arab*   vi, ix, xv, xx, xxi, xxiv–xxviii, xxxi, 38–9, 42, 57–8, 61, 63, 66, 79, 123–4, 132, 134, 138–9
Arkoun   60, 62, 138–9
authority   4, 9, 30–4, 36, 43, 46–9, 54–5, 59, 63, 66, 68, 83, 89, 92, 123, 126, 138
Averroës   xviii, 9, 62, 114, 121

Burke   xii, xxi–xxii, xxxi, 14–18, 20, 26

Caliph*   xv, 31, 69
capitalism   x–xi, xviii, xx–xxii, xxiv–xxv, xxxi, 19–22, 28, 39–41, 65, 72, 85, 133, 136
Christian*   xiv–xv, xxi–xxiii, 5–6, 12, 18, 20, 22, 24–7, 30–2, 36–7, 46, 48–9, 53, 66, 68, 73, 76–7, 94, 120, 125
civilization*   vii, ix–x, xvi, xix, xxvii–xxviii, 6, 32, 39, 41, 59, 61, 66–7, 124, 126, 135, 137–8
communis*   xi, 19–22, 29–30, 65
consciousness   3, 49, 54–5, 87, 91, 93, 131
Copernicus   43–7, 79

critique   ix, xiv–xvi, xix–xxi, xxiii, xxix, 11, 18, 62, 68, 71, 78, 88, 123
culture   ix–x, xii, xiv, xxi, xxv–xxviii, 5–6, 13, 36, 41, 49, 55, 58–60, 63, 66, 71, 85, 91, 122, 124, 136–7, 139

democra*   xix–xx, xxii, xxiv, 16, 28, 30–1, 70, 80, 82, 85
dialectic*   xii, xviii, xx–xxiii, xxv, 29, 41, 115, 134
Divine Law   9, 31, 34, 37, 49, 61, 63, 69, 103–4, 111–12, 116
dogma*   vii, xvi, xix–xx, 9, 12–13, 37, 47–8, 51, 69, 70, 117, 121–2, 124, 137, 139

economic*   xi, xxxi, 16, 28, 38–40, 54, 57–8, 60, 63, 65–6, 71, 75, 80, 136
Egypt   viii, xi, xvi, xviii, 38, 55, 65–8, 70, 118, 120, 127
Enlightenment   xiii, xviii, xix, xxvi, xxxi, 11, 13–14, 16–17, 26, 40–1, 49–52, 60, 69, 120, 123–4, 138
evil   49, 55, 75, 104–6, 108–14, 117–18

freedom   xxvii, 15–16, 33, 40, 51–2, 61, 63–4, 68, 80, 82, 88, 103, 129–30
fundamental*   vii–viii, ix–xiii, xviii–xxv, xxvii–xxix, xxxi, 18–27, 29–30, 32–8, 40–2, 46–7, 58–62, 64–72, 74–80, 82–3, 93, 127

INDEX

good xxviii, 16, 24, 27, 38, 48–9, 55, 73, 75, 88, 104–18
governance xxvi, 31–2, 34, 60, 65, 68–9, 71

histor* viii, xiv–xv, xviii, xx–xxi, xxvi, xxix, 3, 6, 13, 16, 35, 42–3, 50, 54–6, 58, 61–3, 71–2, 74–5, 77, 79, 85, 87, 91, 116–17, 120, 123, 127, 130–1, 135, 138
humanis* xvi, xxii, xxvii–xviii, 23, 68, 80, 82, 89, 139

Ibn Rushd x, xiv–xvii, xxiii, xxv, 9–10, 62, 114–16, 121–3, 126
Ibn Sīnā 5, 10, 112–14
ideolog* xii–xiii, xv–xvi, xix–xxii, xxiv–xxv, xxviii–xxix, 37–8, 48, 58–60, 64–5, 68, 76, 85, 89, 131–4
'ilm al-kalām 12, 66–7
imperialis* xx, xxii–xxiii, xxviii, 134–6
interpretation xii, xv, xxii, xxiv, 9–10, 20, 38, 46–9, 60, 67, 70–1, 81, 87, 90–1, 93, 115–16, 121–2, 132, 137
Islam* ix, xii–xv, xvii, xx–xxi, xxiii–xxiv, xxvi, xxviii, 12–13, 30–7, 40, 58–71, 73–8, 92, 94, 103, 108, 116, 118, 121–7, 129, 131, 134–9

Jew* xiv, 23, 29, 32, 35–7, 55, 73, 94

Kant 11–13, 49, 52, 78, 87, 123, 130
knowledge xx, xxiv–xxv, 4, 7–9, 11, 13, 34, 40, 56, 72–6, 81, 83–4, 86, 105–6, 111–12, 121, 125, 131–2, 134

Maududi 30–2, 65, 70
Middle East 36, 39, 57–8, 78, 82
mind vii, xx, 7, 11, 14, 17, 26, 39, 41, 62, 76–80, 86–8, 92–3, 105, 107, 121, 124, 127–30, 132–3, 139
modern* xii, xix, xxvi, 5, 7, 30, 40, 43, 55–6, 59–61, 66–7, 70, 80–1, 83–90, 92–3, 124–7, 132–4, 138
moral* xxiv–xxv, 15–17, 20, 23, 25–6, 31, 36, 54, 60, 62, 72–6, 80–1, 104–5, 107, 110, 114, 123, 128, 130
Muslim* xiv–xv, xvii, xxii–xxiii, 10, 33–5, 59–61, 63, 65, 68–70, 76, 78, 109, 123–6, 136–8
Muslim Brotherhood xvii, 65, 68–70, 117, 126

New Right xi, xxv, 24–5, 28

organic relationship x–xii, xxiii, xxxi, 40, 47, 93

parasitic x–xi, xx–xxii, xxiv, xxxi, 38, 41
politic* viii, xi, xviii–xix, xxi, xxiii–xxiv, xxix, 5, 9, 11, 14–16, 19–22, 24–5, 27, 29–31, 34, 43, 54–6, 60, 63, 66–71, 75, 77, 80, 85, 95, 110–11, 114, 122–3, 126, 133, 138–9
postmodern* xii–xiii, xvi, xviii–xxi, xxiv–xxvi, 84–5, 89–93
power xii, xxiii, xxiv, 16, 20–1, 27, 34, 39, 43, 52, 55, 64, 83, 85, 117
progress vii, xiii, 13, 15–17, 19, 40, 52, 60–3, 85, 87, 110, 125, 137

Qur'ān   61, 70, 118, 125, 136–7
Qutb   xii, 30, 32–3, 41, 65, 70

reason*   xvii, xxii, 9–11, 13, 16, 39, 41, 47, 52, 68, 73, 78, 81–2, 88, 93, 104–7, 109–11, 115–17, 121–3, 125, 127, 129–30, 134, 135, 137–9
relativ*   vii, xxiii–xxiv, 8, 11–12, 32, 34, 37, 56, 64, 78–9, 86, 113
religio*   ix–xiv, xvii, xix–xxiv, xxxi, 3–7, 9, 11, 13, 16, 18–20, 27, 30, 32–3, 35–41, 43, 46–7, 53–7, 59, 61–4, 66–9, 71–6, 79–82, 87, 92–4, 106, 109, 117, 120–4, 126, 129–31, 138–9
revolution   xii, xxii, xxxi, 4, 10, 14, 20, 26, 37, 39, 41, 43–5, 52, 59, 65, 79, 136

Salaf*   61, 69–70, 137–8
science   viii, xxii, 4, 6, 8, 12–13, 19, 30, 36–42, 47, 54–5, 61–2, 66–7, 72, 74–5, 79–82, 85, 110, 125–8, 130–3, 137
secular*   vii–viii, xii–xvi, xviii–xxi, xxii–xxv, xxviii–xxix, xxxi, 11, 23, 31–3, 39, 42–3, 47–9, 52–64, 66–8, 71–2, 78–80, 82–3, 85, 115–17, 122–4, 126, 137, 139

skeptic*   9, 81, 90, 92
socialis*   xxii, xxiv, 20–1, 23, 29, 70, 72, 130–1, 133
State   xiii, xviii, xx, xxvi, 4, 11, 15–17, 19, 23, 27, 31, 35, 39, 55, 59, 63, 77, 80, 87, 122, 126

theolog*   xiii–xiv, xxiii, 11–12, 18–19, 23, 37, 42, 53–4, 62, 66, 80, 103, 106, 109, 114–16
tradition   ix, xv, xx–xxi, xxiv, xxviii, 4, 15–17, 23, 31–2, 38, 40, 46, 53, 55, 59–60, 62–3, 66–7, 70–1, 75, 81, 83–4, 89, 95, 117, 124–5, 129, 132, 138–9

Viguerie   20–1, 24–8
vision   vii–viii, x, xix–xx, xxv, xxvii, 3–5, 14, 36–7, 39–40, 43, 47, 54–5, 68, 70, 130

Wahhab*   xvii, xxv, 65, 69–70
West*   ix–x, xvi, xxv, 21, 31–2, 53, 55, 59–60, 63, 66–8, 76–8, 80, 85, 91, 124–5, 129, 137–8
world   vi, ix–xi, xv, xvii, xviii–xxi, xxv, xxvii, xxix, 3–5, 7, 14, 20–2, 28, 30, 32, 36–7, 39–44, 46, 52–6, 58–9, 64, 66, 76–7, 79–81, 83, 85, 87, 90–3, 110, 123–7, 129–30, 132–3, 135–6

www.ingramcontent.com/pod-product-compliance
Lightning Source LLC
Chambersburg PA
CBHW061838300426
44115CB00013B/2437